THE SHADE OF HIS HAND

THE SHADE OF
HIS HAND

Prayers and readings
for times of sorrow
and times of joy

MICHAEL HOLLINGS
and
ETTA GULLICK

HODDER AND STOUGHTON
LONDON · SYDNEY · AUCKLAND · TORONTO

'Is my gloom, after all,
Shade of His hand, outstretched caressingly?'

from The Hound of Heaven
by Francis Thompson
(1859–1907)

CONTENTS

INTRODUCTION

The world we live in is the world we live in. There may be times when 'other worlds' will be lived in, and there may even be other people living there, but for all practical purposes we are in the world we know with lands, continents, mountains and oceans. We can work to the future, we can picture and dream and think spatially, but today we live in human bodies with a limited life span which itself is unknown because each of us is going along our particular life pattern for the first time.

Into this life there comes for each of us a variety of experience which runs from joyous to anguished, from brimful to empty, from being loved to being hated or ignored.

One of the aspects or experiences of living from which we cannot completely escape is what is usually called 'the problem of pain'. This itself is divisible into many parts according to our collective nature and individual experience, going from life through death to new life.

Because it is so common an experience, a great deal about it is written, spoken of and studied in the press, on films, and TV, in books, in religion, in philosophy, in medicine. And in the long run, it is still there with us a little alleviated, the frontiers of pain pushed back a little, but not to be forgotten, not to be ignored, not to be banished.

What we have thought about, prayed about and now put before you is a book which meets pain, loss, death, sorrow in a wondering way as we experience it or feel it felt, or see it expressed in the prayers and writings of others.

For us, the great reality which gives a dimension of understanding is the reality of God and the understanding of

1

God in man's life which we learn from Jesus Christ. For us then the study of Jesus in his joy and sorrow, but particularly in his death and new life is a daily necessity if the living of our life and the dying of our death are to have the depth of meaning and purpose which God intends for his human partners of his creation.

We do not pretend to special knowledge and we always hope your experience of God will go further than ours. But what we have wanted to do has been to raise a corner of the black blind of pain, separation and death. This is partly done by facing ourselves and our existence in a beautiful but painful world. It is partly done by verbalising and further living through our own particular, immediate and personal sorrow, loss or bewilderment: and it is partly by encouraging deeper awareness of God and closeness in the Spirit to the love of Jesus.

We do not then seek to give you answers but to lead you into the love of God who so loved the world that he sent his Son. 'In this we know the love of God, that he has first loved us.'

We would like to thank the several friends who have written prayers specially for this book. Their names or initials are under the prayers which they composed. The prayers that have no attribution are ours.

We very much hope that these prayers will be of some help to you.

Candlemas
The Presentation of the Lord   Etta Gullick
2nd February 1973   Michael Hollings

THE WAY

IF I BE LIFTED UP I WILL DRAW ALL MEN UNTO ME

The paradox or seeming contradiction which we face as we begin these prayers is the paradox that it is the suffering, despised, mutilated and dying Christ, who, raised up, draws all men to him. In a way, we should go no further, but simply stand awed, open, questioning and loving before the crucified Christ for a long, long time.

This should be real awe and real questioning, because it is a nightmare for us when we are cut by pain. How then can he attract and draw us?

The glimmering of an answer comes, and only as a glimmering soon lost, when we open ourselves, and do not cringe or curl inwards at the thought or experience of suffering. Look up on the raised one, Jesus.

For us there is another—sometimes a blinding—ray of light, the resurrection, for without that understanding our preaching would be vain.

If I be lifted up

He is despised and rejected of men; a man of sorrows, and acquainted with grief: and we hid as it were our faces from him; he was despised, and we esteemed him not.

Surely he has borne our griefs, and carried our sorrows: yet we did esteem him stricken, smitten of God, and afflicted.

3

But he was wounded for our transgressions, he was bruised for our iniquities: the chastisement of our peace was upon him; and with his stripes we are healed.

All we like sheep have gone astray; we have turned everyone to his own way; and the Lord hath laid on him the iniquity of us all.

He was oppressed, and he was afflicted, yet he opened not his mouth: he is brought as a lamb to the slaughter, and as a sheep before her shearers is dumb, so he openeth not his mouth.

He was taken from prison and from judgment: and who shall declare his generation? For he was cut off out of the land of the living: for the transgression of my people was he stricken.

And he made his grave with the wicked, and with the rich in his death; because he had done no violence, neither was any deceit in his mouth.

Isaiah 53

Lord, you who are lifted up will draw us all to you if we but raise our eyes to look at you and open our hearts to your love. Lord, we all suffer in some way or other; every lover suffers, the sick, the sorrowing, the humiliated, the lonely, the despairing, the depressed are all in pain. But we are all so occupied by our own misery that we cannot lift our eyes to you who would draw us with bonds of love. Lord, turn our eyes from our own pain and sorrow so that we may share our distress and that of others with you and by so doing may be lifted up to you. The sufferings and joys of our crosses will be transformed by your overwhelming love, and we will be exhalted and truly rise to live with you for ever.

You know, Christ, it just isn't so! You said if you were lifted up, you'd draw all men to you. And it just isn't so!

4

Some you frighten off; they think it is ghastly and inhuman, they hate the death penalty and think you shouldn't have submitted. Others couldn't care less; you are so long dead, you're irrelevant. It's only the few that are drawn, and they often don't know why. It isn't an easy job you've got, drawing them. So what are you going to do about it, Christ? If you can't win, how can we win our children, our friends, the rest of the world? Give us a lead! And I suppose you say you have, by forgiving, by continuing to love, by rising from the dead, by continuing to love, by sending your disciples out, by continuing to love, by being always present, by continuing to love. So in the end I expect you'll win everyone, only just give us some hope now, please.

What is the power of your cross, Jesus? It is brutal, sadistic and thoroughly horrible and yet it has drawn men and women to you like a magnet with far greater power than the sugar-like image of your gentleness. You have touched the cross with your love and you have turned it from an instrument of torture into a symbol of hope.

On the cross I see you as Jesus abandoned; help me to see you in men and women who suffer, and to minister to you in them. There is no other way to your heart, Jesus, except through your cross, and when I fully realise this I can feel its pull.

I will never understand your cross as long as I live, but then there are many things I cannot understand. You have given me a heart to love and that is the other part of the magnet, so that if I can only abandon self, it is to you I shall be drawn, and to come to you, Jesus, is to come to your cross.

Colin Stephenson

Lord, the love that lifted you up on the cross draws me to you with an almost irresistible power. Love radiates from your cross and shines on all creation, but so many men do not respond to its pull. Lord, I know that it is a fearful thing to be drawn to you and to rest with you on the cross. Perhaps this is why so many refuse to look at the cross and to accept its redemptive message; they dimly see that they would have to be caught up in this loving and costly self-giving. Lord, even though I may want to escape, never let me cease to be drawn by your love, for in its pain, is peace and joy that passes human understanding.

O Lord Jesu Christ, take us to thyself, draw us with cords to the foot of thy cross; for we have not strength to come, and we know not the way. Thou art mighty to save, and none can separate us from thy love; bring us home to thyself; for we are gone astray. We have wandered; do thou seek us. Under the shadow of thy cross let us live all the rest of our lives, and there we shall be safe.

Frederick Temple (1821-1902)

PAIN AND TRIUMPH OF CHRIST

Was it not right that Christ should suffer and so enter into his glory?

Luke 24.26

Modern life is very full, though some people find it dreary and dull. Few have much time to set aside for quiet, reflection, peace, or prayerful contemplation. But the thesis here is that all these are essential in order to understand and in some measure share the pain and triumph of Christ. If they are not naturally present, each of us has consciously to introduce them into our lives.

It is no good waiting until there is a crisis in life, a sorrow, a suffering or a death. Begin now, if you have not already begun. If you have begun, carry on.

The object we contemplate is a person—Jesus Christ. His whole life and bearing demand our pondering and wondering, but in this particular section we are concentrating on that aspect of him which is all pain; all pain that is, until somehow there encroaches another dimension which seems humanly nonsense—victory, triumph, peace. Such a feeling tends to be present in some of the earlier writers, and later the triumph is lost, so that our generations need to be involved at both levels to obtain a right perspective.

We need to persuade ourselves, firstly, that he was truly man. By that it is meant that he really suffered, he really grieved, he really felt forsaken, he really died. He was a man of sensitivity beyond average, who suffered as much as many, and more than most; a man who, because he is also God, seems to add a dimension to pain that is not realised by us ordinary men and women; yet in this we are not saying he was spared any sufferings of which we are capable, but rather that he entered into such suffering, and suffered it the more intensely. The lives of some holy men and women seem to hint at this, but for many, if not most, it remains dull and unaccepted.

This person of Jesus, closely absorbed into our minds and our whole being through prayer, sacrament and general living, enables us by the power of his Spirit to understand.

Let us open ourselves, and ask God to open us, daily, to his Spirit, so that we may grow in understanding, tolerance and the realisation of the meaning of pain in his life and our own, coming through every tragedy with serenity, every pit of despair with hope, every failure with a sense of his triumph.

The moon was caught in the branches;
Bound by its vow,
My heart was heavy.

Naked against the night
The trees slept! 'Nevertheless,
Not as I will . . . '

The burden remained mine.
They could not hear my call,
And all was silence.

Soon, now, the torches, the kiss;
Soon the grey of dawn
In the Judgement Hall.

What will their love help there?
There, the question is only
If I love them.

Dag Hammarskjöld

Sing, my tongue, how glorious battle
Glorious victory became;
And above the cross, his trophy,
Tell the triumph and the fame:
Tell how he, the earth's Redeemer,
By his death for man o'ercame.

Thirty years fulfilled among us—
Perfect life in low estate—
Born for this, and self-surrendered,
To his passion dedicate,
On the cross the Lamb is lifted,
For his people immolate.

His the nails, the spear, the spitting,
Reed and vinegar and gall:
From his patient body piercéd
Blood and water streaming fall:
Earth and sea and stars and mankind
By that stream are cleansed all.

Faithful Cross above all other,
One and only noble Tree,
None in foliage, none in blossom,
None in fruit compares with thee:
Sweet the wood and sweet the iron,
And thy Lord how sweet is he.

Unto God be laud and honour:
To the Father, to the Son,
To the mighty Spirit, glory—
Ever three and ever One:
Power and glory in the highest
While eternal ages run.

Venantius Fortunatus (c530-609);
translated W. Mair, A. W. Wotherspoon, and
J. Mason Neale

The prophet puts into your mouth the phrase: 'There is no sorrow like my sorrow'. Well, Lord, I challenge that. I am myself, and to me, my sorrow is as great as yours, because it is mine, and it is difficult to see why yours is so bad. I'm sorry, Lord, but that is the way I feel—so you might as well know! Oh, I think I do understand that you are God and man, but then you were able to take sorrow as God and man. I can only take it as I am, just a man, and no one except you and I can know what I suffer or how it compares to your suffering. Of course, in a way I know that you had more to think about and you may have been far more sensitive than I am. But if your sorrow really is greater than mine, I think your strength also is so much greater. Please give me of your strength. Amen.

On the cross, when you asked God why he had forsaken you, what did you really mean?
Were you reciting an old psalm or were you actually conscious of having been forgotten by God in a terribly painful or lost moment of time?
People have said this moment represented the depth of your agony on the cross, a spiritual crucifixion within the physical crucifixion.
Yet you cried out to God. You never felt totally cut off from your father. To me this has always seemed the deepest level of your dialogue with God, your deepest prayer.
Help me to know what you meant here, Lord.

Malcolm Boyd

Behold, I shall relate a marvellous dream which I had in the middle of the night when everyone had gone to rest. I thought that I beheld a wondrous tree borne aloft, enveloped in light, the dazzling cross, the whole vision suffused with gold. Precious stones sparkled from the corners of the earth, reflecting the five on the crossbeam. An angel host, peerless from creation, looked on. Certainly this was no vile gallows; holy saints, men throughout the earth, all this glorious creation, gazed. The cross was glorious, I a wretched sinner filled with guilt.

I saw the shining cross, adorned with streaming banners, effulgent, decked in gold, the Lord's cross magnificently set with jewels. Yet behind that gold I perceived a wretched former agony, when again it bled on that right side. I was troubled with a great sorrow; I was afraid of the wonderful vision. I saw the shining sight changing the colour of its raiment, now bedewed with moisture, now drenched with flowing blood, now adorned with treasure. I lay there sorrowful for a long time watching the cross of the Saviour until I heard it speak. That precious wood began to speak these words: 'It was very long ago—I still remember it— that I was hewn down at the forest's edge and severed from my roots. Strange evil men took me away. They made a spectacle of me, commanded me to hold their criminals. Men carried me on their shoulders and set me on the hill. A gang of evil men fixed me there. Then I saw the Lord of all mankind hasten eagerly to climb upon me. I durst not against God's command bend over or break, when I saw the whole earth's surface tremble. Though I could have struck down all the foes I stood fast and fixed.

The young saviour (who was God almighty) disrobed strong and resolute. He climbed on to the cross bravely, watched by many men, when he suffered to redeem mankind. I trembled as the Lord embraced me. I durst not stoop to the earth nor fall to the ground. I had to stand fast.

11

I was raised up as a cross. I held up the great king, Lord of Heaven. I durst not bow down. They pierced me with dark nails. The gaping wounds can still be seen, visible scars; yet I could not injure them. They reviled us both together. I was sprinkled with blood flowing from his side. After the spirit left him I endured many terrible experiences on that hill. I saw the Lord of Hosts cruelly outstretched. Darkness shrouded the Lord's body with clouds, blackness covered his radiant beauty, darkness settled. All creation wept, lamenting the death of their king. Christ was on the Rood; yet men hastened from afar to their Prince. I beheld it all. I was oppressed with grief and sorrow, but I humbly bowed for men to reach up. They took their almighty God. He was removed from that grievous torment. The soldiers left me standing there, moisture drenched, sorely wounded with staves. They laid down his weary limbs. They stood at the head of the body, and saw there the Lord of heaven. He rested there a while, exhausted after that great agony. They began to make a tomb there for him, in the sight of the slayer. They carved it from shining stone. The victorious Lord was set within. They sang dirges for him, watched at that eventide, then departed weary from their illustrious Lord. He stayed there alone. We three stayed there weeping at that place for a long time after the voices of the soldiers died away. The body grew cold, that beautiful temple.

Then men began to cut us down. That was a terrible experience. They buried us in a deep pit, but friends and followers of the Lord found where I was, and decked me with gold and silver. Now, dear warrior, you might understand that I have suffered the deeds of wicked men and grievous sorrow. Now the time has come that far and wide on earth men honour me. All this great and glorious creation offers prayers to this token. On me the Son of God once suffered; henceforth I tower glorious under heaven. I can heal all those in awe of me. Long ago I became the severest of punishments, a hateful thing, until I opened the right way of life for men. Then that glorious

Prince honoured me, the king of heaven, placed me above all other trees of the forest, just as almighty God honoured Mary herself, who was his mother, above all women.'

Now, my dear soldier, I command you to tell mankind of this vision, that this is the glorious cross, on which almighty God suffered cruelly for the sins of man, and for the deeds of Adam long ago. There he tasted death, yet rose again—his great might to save mankind. He ascended into heaven. He will come again into this world to visit mankind on the day of Judgment. The Saviour himself, almighty God with his angels, will then judge and pass his verdict on each one, as he shall deserve from this transitory life. Nor shall any be fearless for the words the Lord shall utter. Before all he shall ask where is there a man to suffer bitter death for God's name as he did on the cross. Then shall they be afraid and few will know what to say to Christ. But none need fear if he bears the heavenly token on his breast. He that seeketh union with God may attain heaven through the cross from this earth.

I eagerly prayed to that cross with a joyful heart, alone where I was. My spirit ached to leave, and longed for him. Resorting to the cross is the joy of my life, now that I alone am in a more favourable position for adoring it than other men. My heart yearns for it, and I look to the Rood for support. I do not have many noble friends on earth; they have departed from earth's joys to the King of Glory. They now live with the Father in heaven, and dwell in glory. I every day await the Saviour's cross, which here on earth I once beheld. That it may fetch me from this fleeting life and take me to the great joy and bliss of heaven where the Lord's hosts sit at their banquet, that I may be set to dwell afterwards in perpetual joy and dwell in glory in lasting bliss with the saints near the Saviour who once suffered on the cross on earth for sins of men. He gave us life and our heavenly dwelling and restored our hope with glory and bliss for those who suffered hell. The Son was the mighty victor of that successful and victorious expedition. He came

13

with a multitude of spirits to God's kingdom, to bliss with
the angels and the souls of all that dwelt already in glory in
heaven. There Almighty God had come, there his house is.

*c. 8th century translated from Anglo-Saxon
by Mary Gullick*

God How is it you is so brave?
Hezdrel* Caize we got faith, dat's why!
God Faith? In who?
Hezdrel In our dear Lawd God.
God But God say he abandoned ev'one down yere.
Hezdrel Who say dat? Who dare say dat of de Lawd God of
Hosea?
God Who's he?
Hezdrel De God of mercy.
God How you s'pose Hosea found dat mercy?
Hezdrel De only way he could find it. De only way I found
it. De only way anyone kin find it.
God How's dat?
Hezdrel Through sufferin'.
. . . at the end of this play God says to Gabriel:
God Did he mean dat even God must suffer?
In the distance a voice cries: Oh, look at him! Oh, look, dey
goin' to make him carry it up dat high hill! Dey goin' to
nail him to it! Oh, dats a terrible burden for one man to
carry!
*God rises and murmurs 'Yes' as if in recognition. The
heavenly beings have been watching closely, and now, seeing
him smile gently, draw back relieved. All the angels burst into
'Hallelujah, King Jesus'. God continues to smile as the
lights fade.*

Marc Connelly

---

* Hezdrel, in *The Green Pastures* is a heroic leader who encourages his followers to
resist Herod who wants to burn the Temple.

Ecce Homo

Whose is this horrifying face,
This putrid flesh, discoloured, flayed,
Fed on by flies, scorched by the sun?
Whose are these hollow red-filmed eyes
And thorn-spiked head and spear-stuck side?
Behold the Man: He is Man's Son.

Forget the legend, tear the decent veil
That cowardice or interest devised
To make their mortal enemy a friend,
To hide the bitter truth all His wounds tell,
Lest the great scandal be no more disguised:
He is in agony till the world's end,

And we must never sleep during that time!
He is suspended on that cross-tree now
And we are onlookers at the crime,
Callous contemporaries of the slow
Torture of God. Here is the hill
Made ghastly by His spattered blood.

Whereon He hangs and suffers still:
See, the centurions wear riding-boots,
Black shirts and badges and peaked caps,
Greet one another with raised-arm salutes;
They have cold eyes, unsmiling lips;
Yet these His brothers know not what they do.

And on his either side hang dead
A labourer and factory hand,
Or one is maybe a lynched Jew
And one a Negro or a Red,
Coolie or Ethiopian, Irishman,
Spaniard or German democrat.

Behind His lolling head the sky
Glares like a fiery cataract
Red with the murders of two thousand years
Committed in His name and by
Crusaders, Christian warriors
Defending faith and property.

Amid the plain beneath His transfixed hands,
Exuding darkness as indelible
As guilty stains, fanned by funereal
And lurid airs, besieged by drifting sands
And clefted landslides our about-to-be
Bombed and abandoned cities stand.

He who wept for Jerusalem
Now sees His prophecy extend
Across the greatest cities of the world,
A guilty panic reason cannot stem
Rising to raze them all as He foretold;
And He must watch this drama to the end.

Not from a monstrance silver-wrought,
But from a tree of human pain,
Redeem our sterile misery,
Christ of Revolution and of Poetry,
That man's longing journey through the night
May not have been in vain.

David Gascoyne

Of course he had two wills. He had the will of a man,
or even, we may say, the will of an animal, the will to live:
the horror of death, the detestation of pain. And this will
he could not silence for a moment, for it lived in every
inch of quivering flesh, it screamed in every tortured nerve.
In the garden overnight he had done all a man can do
beforehand, to give his will away. He had prayed earnestly,

16

until his sweat ran down: 'If this bitter cup cannot pass me without my drinking it, then, Father, not my will but thine be done'. But no one, not Christ himself, can do his dying beforehand; death cannot be died till it comes, not agony be borne till it seizes us; and when it came to it, all his animal will cried out against the nails. Yet he had another will, the will which embraced his Father's will, so that his Father's will and his were one: the will of the Son of God; the will to drink his bitter cup to the dregs; not because it was bitter, but because it was our salvation.

Austin Farrer (1904-1968)

Lord, in your last journey upon this cross, you have redeemed us,
   this journey of unspeakable pain,
   borne with the memories of Nazareth, Galilee and
   Bethany,
   in this place so starkly hostile;
   and now, Lord, you drink the last of the draught,
   the death of Man, the last heart-beat, the loss
   of pain in oblivion.
   This is death, and here there is no terror;
   in faith
   and obedience you came to this cross,
   endured all its pain, and now in faith
   You die.
You are laying down your life, Lord, trusting in him who is
   able to
   raise the dead to life,
     to bring victory out of defeat,
       incorruption out of corruption,
       honour out of dishonour,
       immortality out of mortality,
       life out of death,
   the God of Abraham, Isaac, and Jacob,

the God of the living and the
dead, the God who raises the fallen.
You are dying, Lord, believing that resurrection is the
last word and not death,
that you will again break bread in the upper room
with your disciples, with the eleven,
and with the countless millions who
shall be their heirs in
all generations;
that you will walk again with the disillusioned and
perplexed, and
Your words will be like fire banishing the
chill of unbelief;
that the church, to be brought to birth by
Your Spirit at Pentecost,
will celebrate cross and resurrection,
the death and the unending life,
knowing the joy of your presence
among men.
Lord Jesus, our dying and our death are yet to come, and
how they shall
come, or when, we know not;
we may pray now that we may not be afraid, but
our faith
is not always strong enough to say
that we shall not be,
we hope we may have courage to bear whatever may be
the ills of our
last journey, but we know our own
cowardice;
our humanity shrinks from pain and
sudden shock.
This life we know, but the next . . .? Our cracked city
pavements
are more sure signs of reality
to us than streets paved
with gold.

Lord, you we know, and in you the Father;
    teach us, Lord, that this is enough, for this
    is life—
        to know the one true God,
        and Jesus Christ whom he has sent;
        may we, day by day, commend our spirits into
        Your hands,
            commend our work and responsibilities,
            our homes and families,
            our loves so precious and so vulnerable,
            our dreams and our hopes,
            our life among men,
            our responsibility to our neighbour here
            and beyond our sight across
                the world:
            that when our last day comes
                we may know
            those hands into
            which death delivers us, as the
            hands which have carried us
            throughout our lives.
Lord, into your hands we commend our spirits
    For he who raised up our Lord Jesus from the dead
    Shall raise us up also, and freely with him, give
us all things.
    Brethren, the Lord is risen!
    He is risen indeed!

Michael Walker

CRUCIFIXION

He humbled himself and became obedient unto death,
even the death of the cross.

Philippians 2. 8

As we have already said, it is important when facing the death of Christ to impress upon ourselves that he died. This may seem a strange and obvious, even stupid statement, but it is easy unconsciously to pass over the suffering and death rather quickly, because it repels us.

Moreover, in the flesh, anyone who has watched a well-loved person suffering *in extremis* must have felt torn between wanting to hold them in life (selfishly?) and wishing it all over, suffering ended and them released.

Even if we consider that we are fairly spiritual, we would be less than human if, with anyone we know and love, we were completely detached about the alternative for them of living or dying.

Christ suffered vilely on the cross, and was tortured as was the custom in those days. His mother and some of his followers actually stood and watched it happen.

And he was a real man, really dying in agony; caused to die by his fellow men in the prime of life. All our human sense of pity cries out: 'He died too young!' 'He did not deserve death!' And so on.

At the same time it is a challenge to us, for as he says, he draws men to him on the cross.

In what sense am I prepared to accept his crucifixion for love of me, and mine for love of him? How seriously do I enter the contract with him, to take up my cross and follow him?

Lord, thou goest forth alone to thy sacrifice: thou dost offer thyself to death, whom thou art come to destroy. What can we miserable sinners plead, who know that for the deeds that we have done thou dost atone? Ours is the guilt, Lord: why then must thou suffer torture for our sins? Make our hearts so to share in thy passion, that our fellow-suffering may invite thy mercy. This is that night of tears, and the three days' eventide of sadness, until the day break with the risen Christ, and with joy to those that mourn. May we so suffer with thee, Lord, that we may be partakers of thy glory, and our three days' mourning shall pass away and become thine Easter joy.

> *Peter Abelard (1079-1142); one of the collection of ninety-three hymns he composed at the request of Héloise after she had become Abbess of the Paraclete.*

There is a distinction between suffering and rejection. Had he only suffered, Jesus might have been applauded as the Messiah. All the sympathy and admiration of the world might have been focused on his passion. It could have been viewed as a tragedy with its own intrinsic value, dignity and honour. But in the passion Jesus is a rejected Messiah. His rejection robs the passion of its halo of glory. It must be a passion without honour. Suffering and rejection sum up the whole cross of Jesus. To die on the cross means to die despised and rejected of men. Suffering and rejection are laid on Jesus as a divine necessity . . .

Jesus made it clear beyond all doubt that the 'must' of suffering applies to his disciples no less than to himself. Just as Christ is Christ only in virtue of his suffering and rejection, so the disciple is a disciple only in so far as he shares his Lord's suffering and rejection and crucifixion. Discipleship means adherence to the person of Jesus, and therefore

21

submission to the law of Christ which is the law of the cross . . .

'If any man would come after me, let him deny himself.' The disciple must say to himself the same words Peter said of Christ when he denied him: 'I know not this man.' Self-denial is never just a series of isolated acts of mortification or asceticism. It is not suicide, for there is an element of self-will even in that. To deny oneself is to be aware only of Christ and no more of self, to see only him who goes before and no more the road which is too hard for us. Once more, all that self-denial can say is: 'He leads the way, keep close to him.'

Dietrich Bonhoeffer (1906-1945)

They forsook him and fled

Did it hurt when they all ran away? And did it hurt when they scourged you? Did it hurt when they crowned you with thorns? And did it hurt when you fell by the way? Did it hurt when they stripped you? Did it hurt when they nailed you to the cross? Did it hurt when they mocked you and did it hurt to see your mother there?

Oh silly, silly questioner. Of course it did, because I was born into this world a man and died a man. So I lived a man and it hurts a man to lose his friends. O yes, it hurt. O yes, it hurt my friend. I knew all pain, from head to toe, inside and out.

And therefore when you ask this question, think hard if you believe in me—that I am God and that I am man, that I lived and suffered and died, because I loved. And now I live anew. And so it is my turn to ask a question, man. Do you believe all this? Do you?

Behold the man

Pilate stood you there, Lord, bedraggled from beating, spit and dirt, crowned with a mocking bunch of thorns, despised, yet by some of the crowd still timidly loved and admired. Now they stand you up all over the place, Jesus. Behold the Jew, behold the negro, behold the Arab, behold the white man, behold the alien, behold the stranger, behold the criminal, behold the believer, behold the clean liver, behold the honest man, behold the man who is true to his love, behold the good man; the crowd call out again: 'Crucify him'. Oh God, when will we ever learn?

Judas

Sometimes, Jesus, I think I understand the torn-pain of Judas. It seems to me he loved you very deeply, but he loved you in the wrong way. Perhaps he was really very close to you, admired you, and wanted so much to be accepted by you. Perhaps he was intelligent and loveable and a bit pushing; perhaps he wanted to push you hard, to tell you what to do, to organise you and your love. And so it went wrong. Your thoughts were not his and he felt rejected, as we human beings so often do. Out of this, I think, grew the need to destroy what he couldn't have. You wouldn't listen to him, you wouldn't go his way, so he destroyed you. And it hurt so much he could not face living. I think I understand, Lord, because I've felt like that; if you won't love me and do what I want, then to hell with you, I'll get on without you for you are no longer mine. Yes, I've felt it and it has gone in deep. And, O Lord, it hurts and it's lonely and then I am lost. It may be silly Lord, but I pray for Judas, because I think I know how he felt. Have mercy, Lord.

I do not know the man

How was it when you heard Peter say that Lord? Were you already numb? Had you caught sight of him already in the crowd with that lift of heart when a friend smiles among hostile faces? Were you hoping against hope he'd give you support, at least acknowledge you? How did you feel? I know I'd be very sore indeed. Not know you! What an awful thing to say. But how like us, Lord, to back away from trouble, even when a friend is involved. Goodness me, your love and your patience when you greeted Peter after the resurrection, and you made him leader of your band. Teach me to suffer loss of friends and to remain myself ready to love and trust no matter what.

I thirst

Such a raging thirst in man, Lord. For you it was physical in pain and dying. No wonder even a cup of cold water is a passport to your Father. But did you not thirst too for understanding, for a glimmer of human hope and response in a world which had deserted you? Did you thirst for the love which you had so freely given to be returned? Did you thirst for the response of God as well as man? What was your thirst, Lord? For I see it in myself, I thirst for you and yet I'm not prepared to be crucified for you as you were for me. I see the thirst in others who desperately need love and understanding. I feel the thirst in the lonely and those who have lost all hope. As I feel it in myself and watch it in you, can you help me to quench the thirst of others from that living water which you promised would flow from the belly?

Father, forgive them

What an extraordinary and wonderful thing to say as you hung upon the cross, Lord Jesus. 'Father forgive them for they know not what they do.' But they did know in one way, didn't they? Just as I know when I hit or hurt or want to kill. I know I still want with part of me to go on, though part of me says stop. And this you knew, Jesus, and you know the cruelty, the indifference, the unfeeling in man. Such a funny creature you brought into being, Lord, such a contradiction of good and bad, humour and hate, love and war. If you can teach me how to know man and what he is, then perhaps I'll learn when I am hurt and almost killed with scorn to say in my heart: 'Father forgive them for they know not what they do.' I hope so, Jesus.

Father, forgive them, for they know not what they do

Lord, to your disciples, that day at Calvary must have seemed
    all darkness and defeat: did it seem like that to you?
    Your hands, carpenter's hands, hands that touched
    the leper and blessed the child, were twisted and
    splintered as they drove in the nails.
    Your body, the temple of God, they stripped and
    stretched out like a bow.
        Did you long to protest your innocence? To
        cry out for justice?
        Did you want to tell the men who crucified you
        that one day they would kneel before you, when
        the sons of God would rise to the new day like
        the great rays of the sun, and all creation kneel in
        the gratitude of the redeemed?

Lord, it was neither your innocence that concerned you,
    nor the resurrection to come that lightened that
    darkness:
        their guilt was your concern,
        it was forgiveness not hope that transfigured that
        moment.

Father, forgive them . . .
    Lord, there are people today who suffer in the
    darkness; who, though innocent, receive violence and

cruelty at the hands of their fellow men.
We pray that the darkness of inhumanity may still be
transfigured by the forgiveness that stems from the
cross.
Father, forgive them:
>the hirelings of all totalitarian systems who seek
>to enslave men's minds;
>all who use power to coerce, to cripple and to
>humiliate those who are weak;
>those who prey upon the fears of others and
>exploit their guilt;
>the cruel ones: the thug, the gossip-monger, the
>aggressively insecure, the thoughtless.

Forgive them, and be the source of all hope, and
light and strength,
to those who suffer at their hands.

For they know not what they do . . .
>That's the terrible thing, Lord, so much evil done with
>so little thought; men who do what they believe is
>their duty, or what is required of them, or what is
>expedient, and in so doing bring guilt upon themselves.
>And Lord, so it is with us. It is easy in church
>to confess to you that we are 'miserable offenders'
>and yet not realise the misery of our offence. It is
>easier to recognise the damage done by the sins of
>others, than to acknowledge our sins for what they
>are.
>When we are vehement and angry in our opinions it is
>because we are afraid that we shall be proved wrong,
>that our pride will fall like Lucifer from heaven;
>our concern is with ourselves and not with truth.
>We use words as if they had no meaning for others,
>we forget the violence of what we say; we chatter
>interminably when we should be silent, and are silent
>when our voices should ring from house tops.

We confess our faith in your forgiveness and yet
harbour resentments month after impious month; we
take umbrage, we have a keen sense of our rights.
We say with our lips: 'Jesus Christ is risen!
Hallelujah!' and we live as if he were dead.

Father, forgive us, for we know not what we do . . .

Michael Walker

Mother, behold thy Son

It was bad enough facing my mother when I had done
something wrong at school. How difficult it would have
been if I had been found guilty in a court of law. I think
against all probability she would have held me guiltless and
loved me still. But with you, Jesus! How did Mary feel?
What was it like for you to have led her to the cross,
through all that worry and anxiety, to know she was watching always just round the corner; humble, silent, loving and
yet surely heart-broken and longing for you to go some
other way? Did you have to let her go through this, was
there no other way? And if the answer is yes, then what do
I learn from that? That I will really suffer deeply if I love
you deeply? That I will get others suffering too? Have I the
right when my faith in you is so rocky? Is that the answer? I
must believe and love more and, then, like Mary, I'll know
how to accept and suffer with you.

Lord, back there in the Garden, in the moment when loyalty
and courage were put to the test, your disciples ran
away; the arrest, the trials, the burdensome march to
this place, you bore alone, without the comfort of
friend, without the support of even one who would

vouch for the truth of your words and testify to what he
had received at your hands.

And now, in this place of cruelty and hostility, these two
dare to stand, knowing that words will not console, nor
pity take away pain, nor love bring you down from the
cross: Mary and John.

Mary who bore you, into whose heart the sword has now
pierced;

Mary who gave birth to and nurtured this body that men
have now broken;

Mary, full of memories—Gabriel, Bethlehem, Nazareth,
kind and faithful Joseph, the laughter of children
playing in the street, the sweet, clean smell of planed
wood, the son she loved whose ways were beyond her
understanding.

John, whom you called from his fishing—was it only
three years ago?

John, as passionate in his hatred as in his love;

John, who understood so much more than the others, yet
even so,
understood so little of the whole truth.

Lord Jesus, the love with which they watch in silence is an
offering that others would make were they here:
they see you, with eyes full of grief, as Bartimaeus
would see you were he here now;
if there were words of sympathy to offer they would
speak them as would stricken men whose tongues
you set free;
they stand sentinel at this cross, as men whose
crooked limbs you straightened would stand were
they here;
they stand—representative of every man, woman and
child
to whom your hands were healing, your presence
blessing,
your words eternal life.

And what they offer, Lord, your words now make holy—
    Mother, son;
    Son, mother;
    you have sanctified the bonds of human love,
    friendship, affection, kindness;
    you have hallowed the frail and vulnerable web of
    human relationships within which our lives are set.

Lord, we accept them every day, the gifts of love that
    others offer us, accept them as if they were ours by
    right, take them with greedy hands with no thought
    of their cost, taking for granted kindness, consideration
    understanding, loyalty, affection and service.

Lord, sometimes we are so obsessed with our own needs
    that we fail to see the needs of others;
    sometimes we use people for our own ends, shoulders
    on which to weep, friends of convenience, statistics of
    our success, useful contacts;
    sometimes we fail in our natural duties to wife,
    husband, brother, sister, mother, father, children,
    lover, friend;
    we stretch their loyalty, strive to mould them in our
    own image, accept what they do for us in our times
    of stress and forget them in theirs.

Lord, touch again all our human loving with your love,
    for in the midst of your agony, you forgot neither
    family nor friend.

Michael Walker

Pain of Mary

I wonder sometimes at the pain of Mary as she stood at the foot of the cross. How could you stand there, Mary? Yet I suppose, how could you go away? The deeper the hurt and injury to the Son you loved, the deeper your own pain: the more he was scoffed at, the more you felt for him: the weaker he became, the more you wanted to support and comfort him. And when he died, you must have felt the supreme dull emptiness of grief and loneliness. I know a little of it, Mary, and because I do, I have to say to your Son —why do you have to let this happen to your mother? It's very hard to understand—yet I suppose this was her glory that you could trust her with everything, even this. Though I'd hate that pain, I wish you could trust me as much.

From the cross

Into your hands I commend my spirit. My God, my God, at this most awful time you seem a long way off. I seem forsaken. My soul is darkened by the fearful mystery of pain and death. I though you would be with me now, but you appear to have forsaken me and my trust in you seems to have been betrayed. Yet I accept this—so be it. You and your purposes alone matter. All is yours; into your hands I commend my spirit.

MAN'S REACTION TO THE SUFFERING OF CHRIST

Are you not the Christ? Save yourself and us as well.

Luke 23. 29

Jesus, remember me when you come into your kingdom.

Luke 23. 42

If you read the Gospels through in an attempt to piece together what attitude was taken to the cross in the time of Christ, you find a widely differing range of human reactions. Peter, even at the mention of suffering and death, tried to stop Christ going to Jerusalem, and was suitably put in his place by Jesus! Most of the apostles fled at the threat of it; Mary and one or two others stood beside the cross, empty, but rejecting, surely hating and surely hurting almost intolerably. The thieves reacted each in his own way, the one implicitly blaming God for everything, particularly for their own plight: the other suddenly knowing how God was loving in the midst of hate!

The variety of reaction has continued down the ages, with emphasis being different according to the theological, devotional, psychological and social pressures of the times. This means that by looking back for expression in writers, saints and mystics we are likely to meet some phrases, prayers and attitudes which strike home to us today, while others are simply alien and even to us distastefully wrong.

Then there is the question of how we ourselves react at the end of the twentieth century when we are living in a strange mixture of callous violence, spiced with mental and physical torture, while at the same time we are abolishing the death penalty and trying to ease pain wherever we can.

Quite simply and humbly, we should look at our reactions, measure them against the reactions of others in the past and try, with the Spirit of Christ aiding us, to allow to grow in ourselves a true perspective of how we should react to the cross personally and in relation to others.

Heavenly Father,
There is a silence in the cross.
When the turmoil dies down we are left
    with nothing but the dreadful deed that has been
    done.
To our lost looking up to heaven there is no answering
    shout.
You portray power in humility,
    strength in weakness,
    dignity in service;
And we did not know that this could be.
Help us find your kingdom as we serve in quietness,
Through Jesus Christ our Lord.

More Contemporary Prayers

To know Jesus is to know God; when we see him we can say to God: 'Now mine eyes seeth thee.' The vision of God in Jesus brings us peace. All is well, we cannot say how, but we are certain of the fact . . . Jesus helps us in our need, not only as the manifestation of God's love, but by his own unshaken faith. He knew the sharp anguish of our lot, faced in all its gloom and terror our bitterest suffering, endured without flinching, desertion, betrayal, torture and death. Even in that darker agony, so awful, so solitary, so mysterious, that we turn dizzy as we gaze into its depths, he called God his Father and said: 'Thy will be done!' . . . If his cross is not the key to the riddle of the universe, it darkens the mystery, and makes the travail of creation more unmeaning than ever. But in the face of all our difficulties it is no easy thing to believe in Jesus. We can realise better now than in some ages how true are the words: 'No man can say Jesus is Lord but in the Holy Spirit.' But when once by the grace of God we have dared to make this great affirmation, then we enter into his unspeakable peace. The world's sorrows do not cease to be terrible, and to wring our hearts, we feel them with all the deeper sympathy and inspired by Christ's Spirit long to relieve them. We understand them but little better, nor can we reconcile them succesfully with the love of God. Mystery still besets behind and before . . . Yet we know in whom we have believed and if we know that, our ignorance is insignificant. That knowledge takes us to the centre, and we find the love that throbs at the heart of creation.

A. S. Peake

Jesus, show me how to link up my pain, my discomfort, my lack of privacy with your passion, and help me to offer these for those who suffer but have little or no faith to help them. Make me like the saints who were glad when suffering came their way because it made them more like you. Teach me not to worry but to leave everything in your hands so that your peace can enfold me. Give me the gift of counsel so that I may know what to do and how to behave day by day; fortitude so that I may have courage and patience when dealing with the small and continuous vexations of life; understanding that I may realise that I am sharing your sufferings though in a very small way; and wisdom so that I may, through you, come closer to your Father both in prayer and in life.

I don't wonder Peter went out and wept bitterly. I have too.

Teach us the cross—
The cross not alone as thy great revelation of love,
But the cross as the way of conquest,
The cross as thy only means of winning thy Kingdom,
The cross as a law eternal of action,
Whereby thy servants must now and for ever abide,
In all that they do for thee,
Or fail and fall:

O Christ,
Royal Christ,
Dying torn on that cross,
Christ, who drank to the bitter dregs
This cup of suffering,
Christ, who saw from afar
That cross, and shunned it not,
But won for us life through its shame and its anguished
      death,
O Christ,
Form in us too this spirit, this will,
Thy cross.

J. S. Hoyland

Judas' reaction was to betray: the apostles' reaction was to
run away: the women's reaction was to gather round to
weep and comfort: the soldiers' reaction was to scoff; the
majority of people just passed by. What is my reaction going
to be, Lord God?

We venerate thy cross, O Lord,
And praise and glorify thy holy resurrection;
For by virtue of thy cross,
Joy has come into the whole world.

Good Friday Liturgy

34

O Lord Christ, Lamb of God, Lord of Lords,
    call us, who are called to be saints,
        along the way of thy cross:
draw us, who would draw nearer our king,
        to the foot of thy cross:
cleanse us, who are not worthy to approach,
        with the pardon of thy cross:
instruct us, the ignorant and blind,
        in the school of thy cross:
arm us, for the battles of holiness,
        by the might of thy cross:
bring us in the fellowship of thy sufferings
        to the victory of thy cross:
and seal us in the kingdom of thy glory
        among the servants of thy cross,
            O crucified Lord;
who with the Father and the Holy Ghost
        livest and reigneth one God
            almighty, eternal,
                world without end.

Eric Milner-White

O, you who weep, come to him who weeps too;
O, you who suffer, come to him who cures;
O, you who fear, come, here he smiles on you;
O, you who die, come to him who endures.

V. Hugo (1802-1885)
'Written at the foot of a Crucifix'

It is extraordinary to sit and look, Lord, not just looking at you on the cross with my eyes, but letting the whole scene penetrate my mind and heart. You teach me so deeply and so gently through your agony, and I begin to know that

35

suffering has a place in the life of the world which I shall never fully understand, but which you explain by saying: 'Come, take up your cross daily and follow me.' This cross is my living, which is joy and pain mixed, misunderstanding and knowledge mixed, loneliness and love mixed. The stretch of your hands reminds me to embrace it all as best I can, even when the very heart goes out of me. Give me courage, give me hope, give me strength.

Lord, here I am at the foot of your cross utterly bewildered by my suffering and by yours. Why should I suffer so much? Why me? I am not very good, but I have not done anything very dreadful. I don't want to hurt others and only want to live peacefully. So why have I to endure so much pain? And why the cross for you? It doesn't make sense. They tell me your resurrection makes a difference to my suffering, but how Lord?

Lord, in your sufferings in the Passion, you did not go outside our ordinary condition. You hallowed real life. Help me to hallow mine. Take my little fears, humiliations and pains, and transform them into part of your sacrifice. I know that I cannot in any way understand suffering until I embrace it and give myself in it to you. It is hard to do this, but your cross can heal the chaos of my life. Give me vision to see you in my pain and strength to hand all of myself to you so that you can transform it into something of worth.

I don't really understand, Lord. It is easy to say that your suffering and death on the cross explains our human pain. For me it doesn't, Lord; at least not just like that. Oh yes, I can see you suffered and I can believe you went through this because of your love. But it is still a real puzzle to me why it was necessary, why it had to be this way. Then I sometimes see how mixed-up mankind brought you to this, and I get a glimmer there of our need and your response. But afterwards I'm off again asking why in that case you made us as we are. I don't think I'll ever understand, but I can see that for me the world is more acceptable in the shadow of the cross and even my own pain now and then seems more of a piece with your vision of life in the world, so I am more at rest. Just let me have the patience and courage to go on looking at you, Jesus, crucified Lord.

Lord, here is your cross.

Your cross! As if it were your cross!

You had no cross and you came to get ours, and all
      through your life, and along the way to Calvary, you
      took upon you, one by one, the sins of the world.

You have to go forward,

And bend,

And suffer.

The cross must be carried.

Lord, you walk on silently; is it true then that there is a
time for speaking and a time for silence?

Is it true that there is a time for struggling and another
      for the silent bearing of our sins and the sins of the
      world?

Lord, I would rather fight the cross; to bear it is hard. The
      more I progress, and the more I see the evil in the
      world, the heavier is the cross on my shoulders.

Lord, help me to understand that the most generous deed is
      nothing unless it is also silently redemptive.

And since you want this long way of the cross for me,

At the dawning of each day, help me to set forth.

Michel Quoist

Not only those who suffer cruelly, like Christ, but all of us, however soft our circumstances to an outward eye, kick at the destiny to which we are tied, and wriggle on the nails of our easy crucifixion. 'If only I were somewhere else—if I were untied from this difficult marriage—if I were released from this routine—if I could be freed from anxiety—if my health did not cramp my spirits—if only . . . then,' we say, not merely, which is obvious, 'I should be more comfortable,' but, 'then I could begin to do something, instead of merely existing'; then, we may even dare to say, 'then I could do something for God.' This is the great deception of the devil, to stop us loving, praying, working, now. It may be God's will you should fight your way out of your misfortunes; it cannot be his will that you should make them a reason to put off living as a child of God.

For the will of the Father stretches from everlasting to everlasting, from before Creation as far as the crown of life in heaven, and there is nowhere a moment that is not carried in the stream of that will, nowhere a point at which he has nothing for us to do, though it be only to wait patiently, or to die faithfully, as Jesus died. No one is free but he who embraces the will of God, and shares in the great energy of love which makes and rules the world. Once we have seen that the will of God, here and now, is our bread and our happiness, what a light, what a liberty, shines on our path.

Austin Farrer (1904-1968)

It isn't any good, it isn't any good! I can't persuade myself of the 'value of suffering'. I think I believe in you, Jesus Christ, But I don't understand you and I can't deep down in me accept fully what you teach. You say you'll draw men to you if you are raised up. Well I just feel repelled; I think the whole thing is repugnant and beastly. I hate the cross in my life and I hate the cross in yours. No, I don't understand and I won't accept. If you want me to understand (and God knows I want to) you'll have to clear away this impenetrable barrier which blocks my view. I so long to grasp and then to live the message, yet at the same time I hate it and run a mile from it. Only you can break the contradiction. Please do, Lord God.

Eternal Father, even as your divine Son, Our Lord Jesus Christ, offers himself to your majesty as holocaust and victim for the human race, even so do I offer myself body and soul to you; do with me what you will; to this end I accept all troubles, mortifications, afflictions, which it shall please you to send me this day. I accept all from your divine will; O my God, may my will ever be conformed to yours!

Abbot Columba Marmion (1858-1923)

When I look at the cross, Lord, I wonder that you hung there. I, who hate suffering so much, look at the image that you have left, suffering accepted and even welcomed as the way through. Did it have to be this way? Would nothing else have answered the nature of man? I suppose I wriggle on the cross and make it worse by non-acceptance. If I wonder long enough, will you let me learn to accept and to forgive?

Jesus is nailed to the cross

Lord, you stretch at full length on the cross.
There.
Without a doubt, it is made for you.
You cover it entirely, and to adhere to it more surely,
    you allow men to nail you carefully to it.
Lord, it was work well done, conscientiously done.
Now you fit your cross exactly, as the mechanic's carefully
    filed parts fit the engineer's blueprint.
There has to be this precision.

Thus, Lord, I must gather my body, my heart, my spirit,
And stretch myself at full length on the cross of the present
   moment.
I haven't the right to choose the wood of my passion.
You present it to me each day, each minute, and I must lie
   on it.
It isn't easy. The present moment is so limited that there is
   no room to turn around.
And yet, Lord, I can meet you nowhere else.
It's there that you await me.
It's there that together we shall save our brothers.

Michel Quoist

Lord, before the mystery of your dying I am silent, dumb.
I do not know what to say or do. All I can do is adore
silently, without words, without even emotion. Yet, Lord,
I want to understand more deeply and love more fully, but
somehow I am empty and drained of feeling. Accept then
my dumb adoration, and the silent offering of myself for
this is all I have to give.

Lord Christ, who didst enter into thy triumph by the hard
and lonely way of the cross, may thy courage and steadfast
loyalty, thy unswerving devotion to the Father's will,
inspire and strengthen us to tread firmly and with joy the
road which love bids us to take, even if it leads through
suffering, misunderstanding, and darkness. We ask it for
thy sake, who for the joy that was set before thee endured
the cross, despising the shame, O Lord, our strength and
our Redeemer.

With All Our Strength

Christ,
    In this dark hour,
Be near,
Be swift to save:
We thank thee for the price which must be paid,
We thank thee for each stab which marks the cost,
We thank thee for all weariness, all pain
Which lays upon us, all too late, our share,
Our share so little of thy cross:
Oh, make us zealous, Lord, to bear, to pay
In secret ways,
That burden and that price:
Oh, give us grace,
That valiantly and uncomplainingly
We may bear on, pay on,
Unto the end,
With thee.

J. S. Hoyland

We are taught in the New Testament that we seek only
because he has found, we beseech him because he first
besought us. The prayer that reached heaven began there
when Christ went forth . . . Our prayer is the answer to
God's. Herein is prayer, not that we prayed him, but that
he first prayed us, in giving his Son to be a propitiation for
us. The heart of the atonement is prayer—Christ's great
self offering to God in the Eternal Spirit . . . Any final
glory of human success or destiny rises from man being
God's continual creation and destined by him for him.
So we pray because we are made for prayer, and God draws
us out by breathing himself in.

P. T. Forsyth (1848-1921)

Jesus, my Jesus,
>> I would be thy servant;
>> trembling I reach to take the cross I must bear, for
>> so thou commandest that such should take up his
>> cross and follow thee.
> Hold thou me up
>> so that in thy love I may bear whatever of suffering,
>> or toil, or hardship, thou mayest appoint.
> I am nothing,
>> my flesh faileth,
>> my heart fainteth,
>> nothing I can bear without thee.

O Jesus, my Jesus,
>> thy love is so great,
>> so wonderful,
>> so precious,
> I would bear all that thou appointest,
>> whatever of trial,
>> whatever of pain,
>> whatever of weariness,
>> if such be thy pleasure,
>> and if each bring me nearer thee.
> Gladly I give thee whatever I can.
>> Thou didst endure the cross, despising the shame;
>> thy hands are outstretched with the marks of thy
>> Passion;
>> thy side is rent with the tokens of love.

Gilbert Shaw

Lord, suffering disturbs me, oppresses me;
I do not understand why you allow it.
Why, Lord?
Why this innocent child who has been moaning for a
   week, horribly burned?
The man who has been dying for three days and three
   nights, calling for his mother?

42

The woman with cancer who in one month seems ten years
older?
This worker fallen from his scaffolding, a broken puppet less
than twenty years old?
This stranger, poor isolated wreck, who is one great sore?
This woman in a cast, lying on a board for more than
thirty years?
Why, Lord?
I don't understand.
Why this suffering in the world
that shocks,
isolates,
revolts,
shatters?
Why this hideous suffering that strikes blindly without
seeming cause?
Falling unjustly on the good, and sparing the evil,
Which seems to withdraw, conquered by science, but comes
back in another form, more powerful and more subtle?
I don't understand.
Suffering is odious and frightens me.
Why these people, Lord, and not others?
Why these and not me?

Son, it is not I, your God, who has willed suffering, it is men.
They have brought it into the world in bringing sin,
Because sin or disorder hurts.
There is for every sin, somewhere in the world and in
time corresponding suffering.
And the more sins there are, the more suffering.

But I came, and I took all your suffering upon me, as I took
all your sin.
I took them and suffered them before you.
I transformed them, I made of them a treasure.
They are still an evil, but an evil with a purpose.
For through your sufferings, I accomplish redemption.

Michel Quoist

*Differences in the contemplation of the cross (A dialogue
between two Brothers in Religion)*

First Brother speaks
>   I flee the cross that doth my heart devour,
>   I cannot bear its ardour and its power.
>   I cannot bear this great and dreadful heat;
>   Far from the cross, from love, on flying feet
>   I haste away; my heart at every beat
>   Consumes me with that burning memory.

Second Brother
>   Brother, why dost thou flee from this delight?
>   This is the joy I yearn for, day and night:
>   Brother, this is but weakness in my sight,
>   To flee from joy and peace so cravenly.

First Brother
>   Brother, I flee, for I am wounded sore,
>   My heart is pierced and sundered to the core;
>   —Thou has not felt the anguish that I bore,
>   Else wouldst thou speak in other words to me.

Second Brother
>   Brother, I find the cross all garlanded,
>   And with its blossoms do I wreathe my head;
>   It wounds me not;—nay, I am comforted;
>   The cross is all delight and joy to me.

First Brother
>   I find it full of arrows sharp, that dart
>   Forth from its side: they reach, they pierce my heart!
>   The Archer aims his shafts that tear and smart;
>   And through my armour he hath wounded me.

44

Second Brother

    I once was blind, but now I see the light;
    Gazing upon the cross I found my sight.
    Beneath the cross my soul is glad and bright;
      Far from the cross, I am in misery.

First Brother

    Not so with me: this Light hath made me blind!
    So fierce the lustre that around me shined,
    My head is giddy, and confused my mind,
      Mine eyes are dazzled that I cannot see.

Second Brother

    Now can I speak, I that was once so dumb;
    'Tis from the cross that all my powers come;
    Yea, by that cross, of Thought and Love the Sum,
      Now can I preach to men full potently.

First Brother

    The cross hath made me dumb, who spoke so well;
    In such a deep abyss my heart doth dwell,
    I cannot speak, and nothing can I tell;
      And none can understand nor talk with me.

Second Brother

    Lo, I was dead, and now new life is mine,
    Life that was given me by the cross divine:
    Yea, parted from the cross, in death I pine,
      Its presence gives me all vitality.

                      Jacopone da Todi (c1228–1306)

I've got to thank you, Lord, for something you have done to me; you've helped me to understand the cross. I've had a terribly empty period when suffering seemed blasphemous and I could not believe you to be a good God with all that pain. Then slowly it has dawned upon me. I cannot put it into words—but I saw you, Jesus, on the cross—yes I saw you for the first time, and now, a little bit, I begin to understand.

I do not deny
that once one becomes a Christian
in every sense,
he just about asks
for crucifixion.

But where there is a calvary
there is an Easter.
Or it is not Calvary at all.
It is just suicide.
The Christian, like the Church itself,
is always growing.
Crucifixion is nothing more
than the cry of breath.
Pilgrim do not be afraid of the cross.
It is a glorious cross.

C. W. Jones

Jesus, I am puzzled by your cross. I do not understand it or you. Are you God or just man? I cannot decide. People keep saying to me that you were just man. I do not know. I repeatedly come to kneel at the foot of your cross, fascinated by it and by you. When I am miserable, overcome by sorrow, or in pain, it is only at the foot of your cross with you that misery, sorrow and pain become bearable. I get drawn into the suffering of the cross and somehow go through the pain to God. Yet I do not know if you, who seem to be the way, are God—the Lord for whom my soul longs and who has been my hope and support all my life. O come quickly to help me, and let me know the answer. I will wait patiently at the foot of the cross.

On finding sweetness in the pain of the cross

. . . It is one thing to come to where the cross is and another thing to find the cross. Trials and vexations are God's ways of bringing us to God's holy place; that is to say, to Jerusalem that is within our souls. But he brought Caiaphas to Jerusalem, and Pilate; yes, they lived in it and were familar with it. You may come to this church where we are and know it; yes, kneel and stand up in it, and say thanks to God for it; and all the while you shall be as far away from that other Jerusalem as Judas was from Christ when he shouldered him in the crowd. The Empress Helena had found a Calvary in her heart before ever she came near it on earth.

Blessed are you if, having come to that Jerusalem, you do indeed find, by God's grace, the secret and hidden thing. For find you the cross without you, you shall find an inestimable treasure, the wood on which our Saviour rested without resting . . . But find you the cross within you, and you shall find Christ himself, Christ that is the cross, and so holy, so sweet, so fresh and fragrant a cross that you should laugh to find how you have mistook him.

This cross is no longer an unwilling sacrifice, no, nor a difficult sacrifice; it is not a slow duty, no, nor a quick duty; not anything at all but our sweet and courteous Lord being to us a justification and a sanctification, and our very life itself; and this is in all of you to be found as surely as the Empress found the wood of the beams in Jerusalem.

Part of the sermon of Thomas Ken from 'Judgement at Chelmsford' by Charles Williams (1886–1945)

Lord, how wonderful it would be to see our pains as yours, to see you in them, bearing them and sweetening them! It is very hard for me to do this now when I am in such agony. When you were on the cross, you knew you were bearing the sins of the world, and there must have been sweetness in that if the pain allowed you to see it. Lord, I cannot think of anything but the suffering and me caught in it; help me to see my suffering as yours and as a sharing of the pains of the world and to find you in it so I may grow more like you. To do this would give a sweetness to the bitterness and messiness of pain; it is not knowing that you are with me that makes it all so very hard.

May your cross support in all times of trouble

O Jesus, mighty King, let your cross be my safeguard, bringing me peace and fullness of life . . . May the thought of your sweet and well-loved cross bring me rest in toil, comfort in trial, healing in sickness, consolation in sadness. May it be the companion of my loneliness, my safeguard in conversation, my light in times of darkness. Let it be my joy through the day and at evening time the theme of my peace.

Thomas à Kempis (1379–1471)

The Way of the Cross

Fill us, Lord, with this pure wish alone,
To spend our lives for others,

To lay them at thy feet
That thou mayest use them for the weary and the lost:

Nought would we ask thee for ourselves,
But only this—O Man of Galilee,
Peasant, outcast, wanderer, felon gibbeted—
That we may follow thee,
May work and suffer valiantly with thee:

Mould us, O Christ,
Beneath thy swift, creative hand,
To do thy will,
To show God's love,
To make his world more free, more joyful
To combat pain and wrong,
To pay, in our own flesh,
Our share of what it costs to help and save.

J. S. Hoyland

Lord, when I have to suffer I get bewildered. Teach me to perceive that if I rebel against pain and think I should not have to put up with it, I will probably become embittered and difficult to live with; but if I live courageously and trustingly through it, I will grow as a person and come closer to you. Help me to endure pain patiently and lovingly for the sake of your Son who did not forgo the pain of the cross, and who could even in his agony forgive his enemies.

It is so obvious, Lord, that we human beings living in this world cannot avoid pain altogether, and no one of us can avoid death. Yet I know I struggle and wriggle and moan against both. It is stupid, isn't it? But what is the answer? Well, even that question is stupid too, as a question.

Because you, Jesus, are the answer, aren't you? You lived, you suffered, you died. It all seemed nonsense, but through it and out of it, you teach us life everlasting in resurrection. Still, I find that hard to grasp as well. How could I ever enjoy suffering or welcome death? In a way, I am certain you did not enjoy suffering or dying, but you did accept. Is it enough in your eyes if I try to accept? I hope so, because even that seems quite impossible at times. As for more than that? I can't do it yet, though I would like to learn the way. Help me now, Lord.

The only thing I can see straight is that you caused your mother and your friends a tremendous grief, anxiety and pain. In a way you got yourself crucified against their desire for you. They didn't get your meaning and it was all too much for them. And yet later, after the realisation of resurrection, it seemed to mean something, so that Paul especially could go out and preach you crucified, and know it meant everything in the resurrection scene. Why can't I see this, if it is true? Can you open my eyes and let me see so that I can bear this unbearable pain. I don't mean get rid of it; just carry it and not pack everything in. Amen.

I had the great privilege, Lord, of kneeling in the garden of Gethsemane, treading the way of the cross and kneeling for long hours on Calvary. At that time I was in a spiritual desert and nothing touched me except the hardness of it all. But I still knew a little of what it meant to be drawn to Calvary, even when a lot of me resisted and twisted. Now years have passed. I look back on those hours from a fuller view and experience of the mingled pain and the joy of living. Faith is deeper since then, love more sincere, or is it mellow? And much of that has come through knowing you, Christ crucified, and letting your cross speak. Go on teaching me, till my own death and resurrection.

Almighty God, who has shown us the true way of blessedness in the life and teaching of thy Son and in his suffering and death, do teach us that the path of love may lead to the cross, and the reward of faithfulness may be a crown of thorns; give us grace to learn these hard lessons, and to take up our cross and follow Christ in the strength of patience and in the constancy of faith. And may we have such fellowship with him in his sorrow, that we may know the secret of his strength and peace, and even in our darkest hour of trial and anguish see the shining of the eternal light; through the same Jesus Christ our Lord.

Author unknown

The wounds you suffered on the cross your disciples recognised in the resurrection. Should I not learn a lesson here? It seems natural that I shrink from being wounded, as you did at Gethsemane. But also I need to recognise that you accepted all that was to come and did not run away. Can you teach me, Lord? And can I learn to greet pain and sorrow and all the natural twists of life with equanimity; and to live through life so that everything is part of development towards resurrection—and most of all death itself. Can you teach me and can I learn that an element of future joyful glory is the right living of the problem of pain now? I'll try to learn, if you teach me, Lord.

Adoration of Christ crucified

Lord, I adore you crucified, lifted up in agony but triumphant. I am dazed by the wonder of it and drawn irresistibly to you. It is strange that gazing at the cross I am overwhelmed by joy. I know that I will have to follow you along paths that will lead to innumerable lesser crucifixions, but because you have shown me the way and are with me, caring for me, there will be always joy and hope mixed with the pain. It is the triumphant love shining from the cross that gives me courage to go on in faith. Never let me lose sight of this vision and never let me cease adoring it, my Lord, and my God.

Pain and triumph

Sometimes—you only know how, Lord—I get a peep into what it may mean to say that you, Jesus Christ, triumphed through suffering, and so triumphed over sin and death. What I mean is that when I can and do bear pain, when I keep smiling and cheerful and caring for others, though I am caught in my own suffering and anxiety and emptiness—then I occasionally feel a lightness, even a joy, an exhilaration, which could be called triumph. Then too, in an inexplicable way, I seem to be able to help others. At least, I am not sure if I help, but they come to me, and they seem to feel it is comforting when I am about. Though I may feel useless and empty myself, they thank me when we part. Thank me for what? I can only think, Lord, that they thank me for the pain and the triumph which was in you, Jesus Christ.

We shall suffer, for the cross is in the heart of God, and in our own hearts too.

A. D. Duncan

The cross

Lord, help me sometimes to stand on the other side of
  the empty tomb, that, understanding Calvary more
  deeply, I may live in the Resurrection more fully:

  there was defeat, Lord, not apparent, short-lived
  defeat, but defeat that must have seemed final,
  permanent and irreversible: the gentle do not inherit
  the earth after all, they are crushed by the powerful;

  there was loneliness, Lord; it should not have been;
  there were eleven who could have watched, but to pain
  was added the loss of friends whose loyalty had been
  promised on oaths stronger than death;

  there was pain, and no telling how long it would
  last; and there was death, to be endured in the faith
  that a resurrection would come; it was to come,
  but first the seed must fall into the ground
  (He was crucified . . . dead . . . buried).

Lord, help me to stand on the other side of the
  empty tomb,
  for that is where some people have to stand:
  those whose cause is defeated, for whom justice
  comes too late to right the unequal balance,
  those who see violence have its way,
  and love kicked aside,
  those for whom pain is not a refining fire,
  a character-building, ennobling experience, but a
  torment bringing fear, loss and bitterness,
  those for whom death is not a consummation, but a
  tragic interruption, an untimely end, a bearer of grief;

  Lord, these know in their bones a Calvary
  I can only know in my imagination and
  in fellowship with them.

Lord, help me to stand on the other side of the
    empty tomb,
    for you stand there now—visiting the souls who
    are in prison (he descended into hell);
    their cause is yours,
    their darkness you have shared,
    their suffering you bear (behold my hands . . .),
    their death you have died,
        and in you, at the last, they shall live.

Lord, help me to stand on the other side of the
    empty tomb . . . sometimes.

Michael Walker

THE TRUTH

GROWING PAINS

Grow in Grace and in the knowledge of our Lord and Saviour Jesus Christ.

2 Peter 3. 18

'Growing pains' is a well-known expression, whether or not it is medically correct. We attribute it not only to physical growth in a young person, but also to the awkwardness and set-backs in the early stages of development in a business, a new committee, a relationship.

It often happens that young people suffer considerably in stages of growth through uncertainty, lack of ability to communicate, and even a positive fear of exposing oneself to another, lest there should not be anything there!

For many who are shy, there is almost an agony in beginning in a new aquaintanceship, getting into a new job, facing a change of living place.

This is a very ordinary pain, and might not even seem worth including in a separate section, if it were not for the fact that understanding and sharing, looking out for and helping are immensely useful in dissipating the feeling of fear in head and stomach.

Once again, it is easy to say and not so easy to do. But the sharing combined with calm awareness of the pain of Christ is good medicine. To face some aloneness without fear gives time for meditating or contemplating Christ's serenity in growth, in making human contact and in winning relationship with most unlikely characters.

It is good to remember how much of Christ's life was 'hidden' life, and in that time 'he grew in wisdom and grace before God and men'.

Do not be afraid to grow, to be open, to be exposed to another and to accept help in growth from God and man. And in your groping, perhaps the thoughts and feelings of others may help a little in the prayers that follow here.

Lord, help us to see in your crucifixion and resurrection an example of how to endure and seemingly to die in the agony and conflict of daily life so that we may live more fully and creatively. You accepted patiently and humbly the rebuffs of human life as well as the tortures of your crucifixion and passion. Help us to accept the pains and conflicts that come to us each day as opportunities to grow as people and become more like you. Enable us to go through them patiently and bravely, trusting that you will support us. Make us realise that it is only by frequent deaths to ourselves and our self-centred desires that we can come to live more fully, for it is only by dying with you that we can rise with you.

Most merciful and gracious Father, I bless and magnify thy name that thou hast adopted me into the inheritance of sons, and hast given me a portion of my elder brother. Thou who are the God of patience and consolation, strengthen me that I may bear the yoke and burden of the Lord, without any uneasy and useless murmurs, and ineffective unwillingness. Lord, I am unable to stand under the cross, unable of myself, but be thou pleased to ease this load by fortifying my spirit, that I may be strongest when I am weakest, and may be able to do and suffer every thing that thou pleasest, through Christ who strengtheneth me. Let me pass through the valley of tears, and the valley of the shadow of death with safety and peace, with a meek spirit, and a sense of the divine mercies, through Jesus Christ. Amen.

Jeremy Taylor (1613–1667)

Lord, help us to grow in 'wisdom and stature' as you did. Help us to use all the difficulties, dangers and pain that come into our lives as means of so growing. When we seem too deeply hurt by the events of life to be able to survive, let alone grow, heal our wounds and give us courage to go on. You only, Lord, can comfort and guide us through all the vicissitudes of life and raise us up when we are brought low.

The brave man suffers injury not for its own sake, but rather as a means to preserve or acquire a deeper, more essential intactness.

Josef Pieper

Trials in daily life

Father,
what happens to us is a great test of character,
and our trials leave us the worse or the better,
depending on how we react to them.
We thank you for Jesus:
he was made perfect through sufferings.

Help us, too, to use our trials and sufferings positively,
to face difficult situations
and to make the best of them.

More Contemporary Prayers

Show me how to bear the pains and upsets of daily life so that like Saint Catherine of Siena I may win something from them, and so grow nearer to you. Help me to see it's no use resenting them. Help me to go through them hopefully and trustingly, supported by your love. To accept meekly is not always the way, often it is right to be brave and go to meet them like Jesus striding out on his way to his death at Jerusalem. Teach me to follow the Spirit in my response to the trials of daily life so that I may become more like Jesus.

Lord Jesus, take my heart and break it: break it not in the way I would like, but in the way you know to be best. And, because it is you who break it, I will not be afraid, for in your hands all is safe and I am safe. Lord, take my heart and give to it your joy, not in the ways I like, but in the ways you know are best, that your joy may be fulfilled in me. So, dear Lord, I am ready to be your servant.

Michael Ramsey

Christ leads me through no darker rooms
    Than he went through before;
He that into God's kingdom comes
    Must enter by this door.

Richard Baxter (1615-1691)

For patience in distress

Give me, Lord, I pray thee, the grace and virtue of constancy, and unwearied endurance, that so I may receive with thanksgiving, whatever thy hand may send of calamity or distress in this life, may bear it patiently, overcome it

58

manfully, and, in every change and chance of life, may, with simple trust and resignation, cast myself and all I have into the arms of thy good Providence. Amen.

Paradise of the Christian Soul

Pain of being hurt by a friend

Lord, help me; I've been hurt by a friend again! I'm full of hate and bitterness and I seem so caught in it that everything that happens makes it worse. Lord, you alone can heal this hurt in me that makes me hate; I seem unable, on my own to escape from it. This hate is so futile for I love her usually; please heal my hurt, Lord.

Pain of love

O Lord, I can't understand why you had to make me love him so much when we can't be together and can't possibly marry. The pain eats into me and makes me utterly miserable. Yet there is wonder and joy in it too, mixed with the agony. But, Lord, physically it is sometimes hell and I don't know what to do about the aching and yearning. Show me how to bear this without becoming neurotic and frustrated. Make this love into something positive and make it flourish in a fruitful and fulfilling way, for you, Lord, are the giver and sustainer of all love, so help me for your Son's sake.

Gracious Lord and sweet Saviour, who sufferest most painful passion for my love, grant me grace most faithfully to follow it.

William Perrin (died 1557)

Pain of loving

Why does loving have so much pain twined in with the joy? It's very odd, Lord. The two go together, whether it's love of you or of a man, or a woman. We get hurt so easily. We think the beloved has forgotten us or doesn't want us. We'd like to believe loving is for ever, but we see people falling out of love, and we know ourselves that we are not worth great love. Loving is a risky business and we are bound to get hurt. Does the pain get sharper and more cutting as love deepens? If so, I am very afraid of it, Lord. Yet the joy and the wonder of loving and being loved far transcends the pain. So, Lord, increase our capacity for loving even if the suffering increases too, and always be the source of our love.

Pain when an affair ends

Lord, the boy I'm gone on won't have anything to do with me now. It hurts so much; nothing makes me forget him. I cry and sob every night and look a mess in the morning, so no one wants me to go out with them. So I sit at home each night feeling miserable; and seeing boys and girls on the telly kissing and necking makes me feel even more lonely. No one wants me. Lord, please help; make me more attractive and bright so my boy-friend will want me again, or so someone will take me out though I feel like a wounded animal that hides away in shame and in fear of being hurt again. O Lord, do show that you at least care, and do something to help.

The pain of the past

Lord, I've been listening in the West Indies to the cry of your people. It is difficult to look back on the past, to know my forefathers enslaved men and women from Africa and baptised them into you while forbidding them marriage and Christian living. I beat my breast, but that is not much good. Lord, teach your rich people in the world how to respect and encourage to come to full living your oppressed people. There is so much destructive pain in hate, so much bitterness to turn new growth sour. Yet out of pain can come purity and wisdom and a vision of a better world, fulfilled in you.

Pain of failing to see God acting in the world

Lord, you said you would be with us always.
Sometimes, when I hear of all the suffering throughout the
    world I wonder if you are still with us.
Are you with the lepers in Africa?
Have you seen the starvation and malnutrition in India?
You have?
Then, why don't you do something about it?
I've read in your books that when you were on earth as a
    man you cured the lame and the blind and the sick;
you raised the dead to life;
you cast out evil spirits.
But now that you have gone from this world as man, you
    don't do these things any more.
Does it make a difference, whether you are here in the flesh
    or in spirit?
To me it does.
You see, now that you are with us in spirit,
I don't know where to look for you.
Must we recognise you in our neighbour?
You've no idea how nasty some of our neighbours can be.
It's so difficult to recognise you in them.
It also implies that my neighbours and friends must
    recognise you in me.
Me! How can anybody recognise you in me!

I am still searching for Christ, the hero.
I cannot find him.
Help me, Lord, to make the world a better place, where I
   will finally find you.

'*Lord make me truly human*': *Teenagers' prayers from
Salisbury, Rhodesia*

Pain of change

Sometimes I feel, Lord, if only I could just stop and
switch off and not go on and on. Everything is always
changing. No sooner am I used to one way, than another
comes along. Lord, is your world going too fast now? It hurts
to pull up roots all the time. Even ideas about you change
so rapidly. Is there no security, or peace, or time to stop
and think? Yet, it's your world and you gave it to us to
bring into fullness. This I know deep down, so I ask you
now for the courage to move on, the patience to accept
people digging me up with new ideas, the love to love them
and their keen movements even when I revolt from change.

When frustrated

Lord, when I complain about the difficulties, the frustra-
tions and knocks that I receive in life, remind me that every
adversity affords an opportunity of learning to rely on you
and of coming to know you more closely. In comfort and
security we can so easily depend too much on ourselves
and material resources, and forget you. Lord, help me to
come to see you in every circumstance of my life and to
trust you utterly.

Pain of being young and insecure

Lord, I am afraid of life. Nothing is secure. I don't know who I am, what I am like, or what I should do with my life. Have I an identity of my own or do I take my colour from my surroundings and become what others expect me to be? I don't know. Violence and lack of cash could shatter my fragile, insecure, little world as well as the greater world around me. I don't know what is right or wrong any more, and no one seems to want to tell me. Everything changes so rapidly. Lord, give me security. Show me how to live, how to find myself and how to know you—if you exist.

Pain of being black

Now, listen here, Lord. You got to do something about these white folks down here. Lord, they giving us a hard time. You got to do something.

Julius Lester

Pain of misunderstanding

I may be only young, Lord, but I see a lot wrong with this world of yours, and your church and the leaders of this country. I get hurt by injustice, by poverty and by oppression. Why are they so blind, Lord, these leaders? Why don't they see they are holding on to what they have got and have no real care for your blind, your oppressed, your poor, your persecuted? Give me patience not to get violent, Lord: give me courage to go on saying what I must say and doing what I must do, even though they knock me. Give me peace in the pain of being despised, laughed at, being told to grow up, being ignored. Lord, teach me how to go on.

Lord, you wanted us to visit the sick, so, answering you, I've been going to her every week. She is very old and sick and blind. She falls about. She is very much alone. At first, Lord, she was so happy and delighted. Now it has all changed. I still go, but she doesn't want me to. She says I am interfering, I'm annoying, I'm after her money. It hurts, Lord, as it did with you when you said: 'how oft would I, and thou wouldst not'. So what next? What shall I do? I'd like just to pack up and leave her to get on with it! But perhaps that's running away—I just don't know. Send your Spirit to show me the way.

Lord, help me to endure the pain of my family's lack of understanding at my wanting to be a doctor. I want so much to be a doctor, and I know I have the ability; you gave me it and the desire to serve you this way, at least I think so. But, Lord, I must get good 'A' levels, and it is so hard to work at home when we are all living in the one room with the telly on the whole time and the family chattering. My teachers don't understand my problems at home and think I am just not up to it. Give me a friend who will understand, and give me strength to persist when everything seems utterly hopeless. I ask this for the sake of your Son.

I thought I was his friend, Lord, and that we understood each other so well. But now he is going off at a tangent on some new political business, radical, revolution, force, disruption, all sorts of things which I cannot take. It's painful to feel the contact disintegrating. He talks at me now, not with me. There is no longer dialogue and similarity. And he may be right, Lord; I may be just old and tired and unwilling to move. So give me the power to listen, the love to care and the openness to understand, even through pain.

Pain of rejection

I need you so much. I am being rejected by my own family and it hurts so deeply. Lord Jesus, you are the only person I know that was completely rejected, so you understand the loneliness, the hurt and the great darkness of rejection. I love them, Lord, but I am not good at expressing my love. Help me to go on loving the way you did when you were rejected. Stop me from saying bitter things which I'll regret. Perhaps then they will see how much I love even though I may not behave the way they want. Lord, don't leave me for I need you so very much.

In a difficult human situation

Lord, I don't want to go through with this frightening thing that lies before me. Can't you get me out of it? Many people look upon you almost as a pain-killer or magician who will help them to evade the horrors and sufferings of human life; but you did not do this for Jesus when he asked for the cup to be removed from him 'if it were possible'. Lord, 'if it is possible' get me out of this; if it is not help me to face up to it and prevent me from running away. I know if you give me strength not to evade it, I can win through to a new life through the suffering, like Jesus did, even though it will mean crucifixion of one sort or another. This way, perhaps, suffering can become something valuable and good, and even lead to peace and joy, and resurrection for me. Lord, help me!

The pain of meeting a sick person

She wrote and told me she had cancer and not to be shocked when I saw her. But Lord, I never guessed. When I saw her two years ago she was a fine, strong woman, beautiful. Now, Lord, she is a bag of bones, her hands like bird's claws, her face shrunken in, her eyes burning with fever. O God, it hurts to see her pain, her struggle to breathe. And Lord, the memory hurts—that she will not walk again, or come out into the garden she loved, or visit the poor, or go to church. It hurts, yet she is still alive, alert, thoughtful, loving, and somehow that makes it hurt more. Help me to help her in love.

Pain of a parent

She just won't listen, Lord. I've tried to be a good mother, to give her all she needs, to help in her education, to love her deeply. And now everything is wrong. She won't listen, she doesn't care, she's got in with such a group of layabouts and drug-takers and the rest. I can't help fearing for her, but if I say anything it simply makes it worse. When I see her appearance and watch her smoke and know she takes drugs, and know she doesn't pray, I ache for her, Lord. It's surely a mother's ache. What must I do then? Do I ever talk? Can I ever correct? O God, I need your guidance.

Agony of living with a neurotic person

Lord, why are you so harsh? Why do you make my life so unbearable? Living with a person who is continually depressed makes my life hell on earth, and her misery is grim too and beyond my understanding. It seems to me that your Son was only in agony on the cross for three hours; my suffering appears to have no ending. Lord, help me. Change the situation, or me, for I am finding it hard to believe you are a loving God. How can you be loving when you leave me in this intolerable misery, giving me no support, no hope? To cease to believe that you are loving would be the most horrible blasphemy, but how can I do otherwise? Help, Lord, help!

Facing trouble

When shall this heart of mine, my God, take up the shield of patience? When shall I, learning to please my Lord, face trouble with untroubled mind?

Lorenzo Scupoli (1529-1610)

I can't take any more disaster, Lord. I'm off!

Pain of trying to understand those society condemns

Lord, I find it very hard to be understanding and compassionate with those who break the law and go against society. Jesus, you endured in your soul the dreadful torments of a condemned and lost man. I am afraid to follow you to the cross and to endure and experience with you the pain of the condemned, and so come to understand the outcasts of society more deeply. In order to love and understand others we must go by the way of the cross, denying ourselves in some deep manner which I can only dimly comprehend. Lord, teach me how I must do this however painful it may be, for I do want to follow you and love you and all people as you would have me love, but I am very blind and need your light and your Spirit.

Pain of indecision

There is a kind of pain, Lord, which I can only describe as dividing. There seem to be two choices open to me. Both seem good and I don't know which to go for. I make up my mind at night to do the one, and in the morning everything has turned head over heels and I am beginning to think I must go the other way. How do I choose? What do you want of me? It really hurts to be indecisive and it can't go on. Is this what it is all about—my freedom; having to stand on my own and decide, being responsible and knowing that I may make the wrong choice, yet having the courage and calmness to come to a decision? So, Lord, I ask you to fill my being with your Spirit of understanding and wisdom. Amen.

When things are desperate

Lord, things are desperate; I can't carry on much longer like this. I am being battered on all sides and don't know what to do. Where are you, Lord? Don't you care? Can't you come into my life in the way that you came into the disciples' boat when they were storm-tossed on the Sea of Galilee? Then your presence changed the situation and brought peace and calmness to them. Do this in my life; by the light of your presence calm my troubled spirit. I don't want things to be easy, but I do want some assurance that you are with me and that you won't let me be destroyed by the batterings of life. I know you won't give me security and that I will have to go muddling on, so give me faith to trust your guidance even though the ways you choose seem mad to me.

Grant, gracious Father, that I may never dispute the reasonableness of thy will, but ever close with it, as the best that can happen. Prepare me always for what thy providence shall bring forth. Let me never murmur, be dejected, or impatient, under any of the troubles of this life, but ever find rest and comfort in this, *this is the will of my Father, and of my God:* grant this for Jesus Christ's sake. Amen.

Thomas Wilson (1663-1755)

O Lord, I fling myself with all my weakness and misery into thy ever-open arms. I know that I am ignorant and much mistaken about myself. Thou, who seest in very truth, look mercifully on me. Lay thy healing hand upon my wounds. Pour the life-giving balm of thy love into my heart. Do for me what I have not the courage to do for myself. Save me in spite of myself. May I be thine; wholly thine, and, at all costs, thine. In humiliation, in poverty, in suffering, in self-abnegation, thine. Thine in the way thou knowest to be most fitting, in order that thou mightest be now and ever mine. Thou art my strength and my Redeemer. I am thy poor little creature, dependent on thy merciful charity alone. Amen.

Charles J. B. Besson (1816-1861)

O God, who makest cheerfulness the companion of strength, but apt to take wings in time of sorrow, we humbly beseech thee that if, in thy sovereign wisdom, thou sendest weakness, yet for thy mercy's sake deny us not the comfort of patience. Lay not more upon us, O heavenly Father, than thou wilt enable us to bear; and, since the fretfulness of our spirit is more hurtful than the heaviness of our burden, grant us that heavenly calmness which comes of owning thy hand in all things, and patience in the trust that thou doest all things well. Amen.

Rowland Williams (1818-1870)

Insecurity

The world is a frightening place, Lord. I look out at it and it scares me. I don't feel secure in your world. I feel so little and everyone and everything is rushing about. There is no peace; people kill and steal and smash and grab. I thought I was secure in my job, but now there is redundancy; I thought I was just catching up on money and everything has shot up in price. Worst of all, Lord, I thought I was secure in my love and even this seems to be fading away. I'm not even convinced about you. Oh, Lord, make something in me feel secure.

In sorrow or in trial

Lord, do not permit my trials to be above my strength; and do thou vouchsafe to be my strength and comfort in the time of trial. Give me grace to take in good part whatever shall befall me, and let my heart acknowledge it to be the Lord's doing, and to come from thy providence, and not by chance. May I receive everything from thy hand with patience and with joy; through Jesus Christ our Lord.

Thomas Wilson (1663-1755)

In sorrow

O Lord God, holy Father, be thou blessed both now and for evermore, because as thou wilt, so is it done, and what thou doest is good. My soul is sorrowful, sometimes, even unto tears; sometimes also my spirit is disquieted, by reason of impending sufferings. I long after the joy of thy peace, the peace of thy children I earnestly crave. If thou give peace, if thou pour into me holy joy, the soul of thy servant shall be full of melody, and shall become devout in thy praise. Make me a dutiful and humble disciple (as thou art wont to be kind), that I may be ever ready to go, if thou dost but beckon to me. Thou knowest what is expedient for my spiritual progress, and how greatly tribulation serves to scour off the rust of sins; do with me according to Thy desired good pleasure. Amen.

Thomas à Kempis (1379-1471)

Sadness

Ah God! behold my grief and care. Fain would I serve Thee with a glad and cheerful countenance, but I cannot do it. However much I fight and struggle against my sadness, I am too weak for this sore conflict. Help me in my weakness, O thou mighty God! and give me thy Holy Spirit to refresh and comfort me in my sorrow. Amid all my fears and griefs I yet know that I am thine in life and death, and that nothing can really part me from thee; neither things present, nor things to come, neither trial, nor fear, nor pain. And therefore, O Lord, I will still trust in thy grace. Thou wilt not send me away unheard. Sooner or later thou wilt lift this burden from my heart, and put a new song in my lips; and I will praise thy goodness, and thank and serve thee here and for evermore. Amen.

S. Scheretz (1584-1639)

In misery

All-seeing light, and eternal life of all things, look upon my misery with thine eyes of mercy, and let thine infinite power vouchsafe to limit out some portion of deliverance unto me, as unto thee shall seem most convenient. But yet, O my God, I yield unto thy will, and joyfully embrace what sorrow thou wilt have me suffer. Only this much let me crave of thee (let my craving, O Lord, be accepted of thee, since even that proceeds from thee)—let me crave even by the noblest title, which in my greatest affliction I may give myself, that I am thy creature, and by thy goodness (which is thyself), that thou wilt suffer some beam of thy majesty so to shine into my mind, that it may still depend confidently on thee. Amen.

Sir Philip Sidney (1554-1586)

Invocation for when in trouble

O Saviour of the world, who by thy Cross and precious blood has redeemed us, save us and help us we humbly beseech you, O Lord.

Sarum Manual

Pain of grief

Lord, we find grief hard to bear,
    sometimes the weight of it grows lighter
        —time heals, they say, but there is a grief for
        which eternity would be too short—
    it belongs not to our present, but to our past,
        without pity it pulls us back along
        the way of memory, habit, familiar things,
        and reminds us of
            what once we had,
            what used to be,
            what is no longer.
And so, Lord, we are driven back to time past,
    to the tomb that houses the dead,
    that was to us warmth, life, kindness, love,
        companionship to keep vigil with our memories,

unbearable, because they are filled with what
no longer exists,
inescapable, because without this burden
we have nothing.
There are tears, Lord,
people say we shouldn't shed them, they expect us to
be composed and brave, to disguise our feelings and
keep them private; tears, they say, are only
upsetting to other people,
—but you have given us tears, Lord,
a sacrament of our bodies,
an outward and visible sign of an
inner and spiritual truth,
an expression of the inexpressible,
saying what our lips cannot say;
tears are the physical, tangible signs that our
grief is to do with flesh and blood, with the
things our eyes have seen, our ears have heard,
our hands have touched.
She came that morning, Lord,
to sit by the tomb, alone with grief,
Mary, whom you forgave, made whole,
raised, blessed;
she came because it seemed that grief could do
only futile things, watch and remember;
soon there would be the last act of love, the
anointing, disguising the stench of death with
fragrance, and, after that, watch and remember;
and through eyes, blinded with tears,
the present had no reality,
the garden could have been a desert,
parched and pitiless, it would have made no
difference,
the gardener could have been anyone,
anyone at all.
Until out of the present
there came the word that filled

that moment with grace
and the future with hope.
Lord, it was such a simple word,
   not a sound of trumpets,
   not a profound word,
      ponderous with learning,
      brilliant with insight,
   it was such a simple word, Lord,
      —you called her name.

Michael Walker

Blackmail

I'm caught, Lord. They are blackmailing me. I know what I did was wrong and they got the hold over me. I know what they are doing and it is destroying me. I can't eat or sleep; I can't concentrate. Lord, I should go to the police and I'm too afraid of their threats. Give me some new courage and humility and trust so that I can take the right steps and not be weak again. Oh God, it can't go on like this, nothing is safe from them. I see what I must do. Give me the guts to do it.

Fear of violence

Lord, I am afraid for I am being threatened by violent men. If I tell the truth about what I saw and ignore them, they will damage my family. What must I do? How can I let my family be hurt in order to help a person I do not know? Yet I know I should tell the truth. Lord, must I risk my family in the hope that the man will be caught before they get at them? Help me, Lord!

Fear of vengeance

Lord, I am afraid for there seems no end to vengeance in the world today. Lord, stop us from ruthlessly taking justice into our own hands, and from demanding even more than one tooth for one tooth, and one eye for one eye. Make us really understand what you meant when you told us to turn the other cheek; help us to realise that this means refraining from hurting mentally and emotionally those who wound us deeply as well as not wishing to kill or injure a Protestant or a Catholic who has slaughtered our nearest and dearest. To do this is very hard so, dear Lord, help us with your Spirit to be loving to both our friends and enemies.

Pain of disunity

The pain of separation is especially great at your supper, Lord. Here if I kneel and pray with my friends and worship you in spirit and truth can your bishops tell me not to receive communion? I don't understand. I just kneel and ache and wonder and pray, but, Lord, it doesn't help my faith.

I think, Lord, very often that if you were incarnate today you'd weep over Rome and Canterbury, Istanbul and Geneva. You'd say between your tears: 'How oft would I —you would not'. Because your Spirit has done so much, given so many chances, opened so many doors, broken down so many barriers and still your church and chapel people sleep on, or worse, they wake up and say: 'No! It's too dangerous, leave us alone.' Then they go to sleep again. God, help us!

Why are we separated at the Eucharist my friends and I? Lord, this is a sad pain which makes me sometimes forget the deep union we experience together in prayer made in your name. Send your Spirit to heal the divisions that rend your body, and Lord heal our pain.

Pain after having been cross with children

Oh God, I was so cross with the children today. Forgive me. Oh God, I was so discouraged, so tired, and so unreasonable, I took it out on them. Forgive me.

Forgive me my bad temper, my impatience, and most of all my yelling.

I cringe to think of it. My heart aches. I want to go down on my knees beside each little bed and wake them up and beg them to forgive me. Only I can't, it would upset them more.

I've got to go on living with the memory of this day. My unjust tirades, the guilty fear in their eyes as they flew about trying to appease me. Thinking it all their fault— my troubles, my disappointments.

Dear God, the utter helplessness of children, their vulnerability before this awful thing, adult power. And how forgiving they are, hugging me so fervently at bedtime, kissing me goodnight.

And all I can do now is to straighten a cover, move a toy out of an upthrust hand, touch a small head burrowed into, and beg in my heart: 'Forgive'.

Lord, in failing these little ones whom you've put into my keeping, I'm failing you. Please let your infinite patience and goodness fill me tomorrow. Stand by me, keep your hand on my shoulder. Don't let me be cross with my children.

Marjorie Holmes

Unable to have a child

Lord, Creator, I have always believed that you are maker of all things and people. I don't really know what that means, but somewhere deep down I feel you keep me going and one day I will meet you in heaven. But the trouble is that we cannot make a baby. We've tried so often, seen so many doctors and yet no child is conceived. It hurts, Lord! Don't you trust us? Would we be such bad parents? Can you understand the pain of not being able to achieve what is so much part of our being? You wept when Jerusalem would not co-operate with you. I weep when you will not co-operate with us. Give us a child to love.

Aging and childless

Lord, I am getting on now. You have never let me have a child, though I've prayed and we've tried. You gave Abraham and Sarah a child when they were old. Scripture says they laughed when you promised they'd bear a child, and you still fulfilled your promise. I'm not laughing, Lord! I ache inside with my longing. But when you let me give birth then I'll laugh, Lord—with joy. Indeed I will!

PARTING

You are sad now,
but I shall see you again, and
your hearts will be full of joy.

John 16.22

Much of life is touched with parting. In the very moment
of our birth we part from our mother's womb. A number of
people spend their lives trying to clamber back in, but most,
however much they hate it, accept a continued measure of
parting as inevitable all through life, and into death.

This is the true and wise and Christian attitude. Let us
admit we do not always manage to live it, but it is better for
you and us and everyone if we face reality as Christ as man
faced it. Life is for living and death is for dying, and we
can say with the conviction of faith, resurrection is for all!

But life is not for running away or hiding your head in
the sands of busyness. We follow Jesus who claimed to be
the way, the truth and the life. And he personally knew
parting in many different shapes. He went through birth
and through death. In between he left home, found he had
no time for his mother and friends, he was so pressed. In a
way, he parted company with 'established' Judaism; felt the
sting of those who 'followed him no more'; accepted the
betrayal by Judas and the failure of his closest friends to
back him up. He knew the parting from those he loved,
Joseph, John the Baptist, his own mother.

But he also set the example of deliberately leaving all and
being left by all. In him again we can find sense and strength
and leadership. Once you have found that example in
thoughtful prayer and listening to the Spirit, you will find
parting just as real, if anything deeper, but somehow
acceptable and even fruitful for you and others.

Remember, when you have learned not to dread parting but to take it in love, you will have a greatly increased work in life among those who have still to learn this. This work of compassion is virtually endless once you have had your eyes and heart opened. But opening is painful and the pain does not, should not, go away; if anything it intensifies with your growing sensitivity, but is liveable in a new and deeper way.

Part in peace: Christ's life was peace,
Let us live our life in Him;
Part in peace: Christ's death was peace,
Let us die our death in Him.

Part in peace: Christ's promise gave
Of a life beyond the grave,
Where all mortal partings cease;
Brothers, sisters, part in peace.

Sarah Flower Adams (1805-1848)

The angel of the Lord appeared to Joseph in a dream and said: 'Get up, take the child and his mother with you, and escape into Egypt, and stay there until I tell you, because Herod intends to search for the child and to do away with him'. So Joseph got up and taking the child and his mother with him left that night for Egypt where he stayed until Herod was dead. This was to fulfil what the Lord had spoken through the prophet: 'I called my son out of Egypt'.

Matthew 2. 13-15

The refugee

Lord God, what have you done to me? I have worked
hard and built up my home and family. I have tried to love
you and serve you in them and in the world. I know I've
often fallen down and not been a good neighbour and not
loved enough. But now, Lord, it is all gone. I'm driven out
of home and country; everything I had is destroyed; we
are not even living together but the family is separated in
different camps. Lord, have mercy on us. Help us.

A lover's parting

My heart is breaking at the thought of this parting. Why
did you let me love him so much when this was going to
happen? Lord, I am afraid that he will forget me and find
someone else to take my place in his life. I am afraid that
I will forget what he looks like and the kind of thing he
says. I know that Dante made hell for the lovers Piero and
Francesca consist in their eternally embracing; life constantly with one person might be a kind of hell, but separation on earth too is a kind of dying. Lord, help me to bear
this kind of death and to always remember that we are
united in you and that this separation is not final. Don't
let us grow too far apart. Let me remember that you will
always be with us, even to the end of the world.

Compulsory move of home

I've lived here all my life, Lord, and now I'm getting on
in years. I know all the streets and all the shops and my
neighbours. But they say they are pulling the place down,
Lord. They've got a road coming through, and the house
has got to go, and I've got to go too. I love it all so much,
it's right in my heart and my bones. And worse than that,

Lord, they will only put me in that new housing estate which is miles from here, and I shan't really know anyone, or the shops or church or anything. O Lord, how cruel men are to each other. Get them to change their plan or something, Lord, my heart is breaking.

The young one parting

I know I've got to go, Lord, I can't stay round home any longer. I've got to be myself and grow and live my life. But it's comfortable here too, Lord, and I'm getting cold feet about moving and it's hurting mother and father a lot, but I must go. Give me the strength and courage.

Away from home, first time

I've never been away before, and now I feel so lonely and so homesick. I'd gladly pack up and creep back home Lord, and yet I suppose I mustn't. The food is so odd, Lord, not like the stuff Mum cooked. The bed is hard, and the rooms noisy with traffic and other people banging doors, other people's radios, which just make me feel more lonely. And you know, Lord, I'm scared of all these other people. They seem so self-assured, they talk loudly to each other, they know what they are doing, and they don't even bother to say hello to me. So I'm a bit lost, Lord, and I don't want to run away, but I'm afraid I might unless you strengthen me.

A daughter at university

I left her at college, Lord, and it was all so new and strange to me. All the young people looking in such a mess, and not noticing us, and talking in language I could not really follow. And then the buildings, so huge and easy to get lost in . . . her nice room. It's really nicer than home, and I hope she'll like it, Lord, and settle in and not meet horrid people, but make good friends; not take to drugs or get pregnant or anything like that. It all seems so open and free-and-easy. I'm scared for her, Lord. And though she must grow and learn, please don't let her grow away from us, get too clever and too grand, and turn up her nose at our poor little place after all this she has here. Oh Lord, you see I have so many worries for her, and I can only pray and leave her to you. Watch over her, Lord.

The pain of parting

Lord, we only met a few weeks ago. Something drew us together and we plunged deeply into thoughts and fears, hopes and previously uncommunicated levels of being. It is difficult to describe because it doesn't happen often. It all seemed so growing, loving, fulfilling and rich. And now we must part, not just a few miles but thousands of miles, different continents. The pain cuts deep, Lord, yet we both know it's right. But that doesn't make it any better. Letters won't really help! Perhaps you will let us grow in the Spirit together on the foundation laid in you and perhaps the very pain will help the growth like pruning, Lord.

Knowing a friendship can't go on

We have tried so hard, Lord, and we have come so close together. But I know it will not work. She says it will and that we should try, but it won't, Lord, and it is much too big a thing to experiment with. I just know we could not go on, and if we did, we might destroy each other. She doesn't see it, and she is bitterly broken. Lord, I hate to hurt her, but surely I must not say 'yes' to heal that hurt, when I'm sure it will only be worse later? Yet how to part without too much hurting? I'm kneeling here asking you because I don't see the way at all. Please give me light.

On the departure of a young member of the family

It had to come, Lord, I know. Ever since the earliest days, she was growing and learning and getting more independent. She was loving and sweet, and we had our ups and downs. But she meant so much to both of us. And now she is off to Australia and perhaps we won't see her again. Make her happy, Lord; make her meet the right man and not be lonely or lost. And, Lord, please let us keep in touch and see her again before we die. I trust her to you, Lord. Keep her safe.

Giving up a boy friend

I suppose I always had the fear it would happen to me, Lord—that I would fall in love and then after a time things would go wrong. And now it has happened, and he has gone off with another girl. He says we can be friends, but it is not like that with me, because, you see, I love him, oh! so much, and it is breaking my heart. I want to pray that he'll come back; and then I want to pray that he will be happy, even if I am not; and then I get swamped and I cry, and I know really I only want selfishly to be happy with him again. So, though in a way I don't really mean it, I'm trying to say it is over to you, Jesus Christ. You knew about love and about parting. Can you see me through in whatever way is best?

Loss of a girl

O God, my heart's bursting, and my pride is shattered, I'm poured out like water and am empty now, except for a mixture of love and hate. Why did she have to make me love her and then do this to me? Can I ever hold my head up again? Can I ever give up loving her, or hating her? Can I ever love anyone again . . . or trust their love? O God, what shall I do?

Leaving a much-loved job

Lord, for more than twenty-five years I've been flying 'planes, then teaching others to fly, and now I'm told I am too old and must have a ground job. It's like dying, Lord, this parting from flying. It was my life, my whole being. Things now seem flat and profitless. Help me to adjust and to find some new interest and challenge. I can't see how his can come about, but perhaps if you will assist me and guide me I will regain my zest for living. Help me, Lord.

Leaving my country

You took me away from my family and friends to work for you and now, Lord, you want me to leave my country which I love so much. This will be a very hard parting. Making the break will wring my heart. I love the hills, the open sky, the sea and the friendly people. Why must I leave them? You are a hard master. I know you said your followers must leave their families to follow you, but somehow for me to leave the country I love is the most cutting of griefs. Support and strengthen me when I make this break, Lord, for I cannot cease to follow you, for without you I am lost.

Parted husband and wife

Lord, I am away from her for six months at the other side of the world. I miss her so. Keep her and the children safe. Keep her loving me and don't let the children forget me. And Lord, guard my eyes and my heart. Don't let me get caught up with any other woman in my loneliness and distance. Keep me true and get us all together again as a loving family soon.

PHYSICAL PAIN

Heirs of God, co-heirs of Christ, sharing his sufferings so
as to share his glory.

Romans 8.17

As each of us is individual and unique, we cannot fully
share an experience of pain with anyone else when suffering
even something as common as a headache, toothache or a
stomach ache. You probably have had all these at some time
in life—we have! We could describe each to you vividly
in word, sound and gesture, but even if we recalled your
pain for you, it would be your pain recalled for you and
ours for us.

Nevertheless, we come close enough to have some
sharing, and so some sympathy; though the less experience
in a particular field, the less easy it is to realise what another
is going through. How can we, who up till now have not
suffered arthritis, know the pain of those we know and love
and often visit who can scarcely stand or move from a
chair? How can we who are not blind sense the pain of
blindness, or the blanket of deafness, the 'dead-body-
weight' of the paraplegic?

So there is that element in trying to share in which we
can only say: 'I know pain' rather than: 'I know your pain'.
Therefore, you see, it is important in the brotherhood of
man that we all, being born into a world of pain, in some
degree experience it too.

Again, what extraordinarily differing effects pain has on
different people. It is one of those pondering points about
pain that it exists at all. But it is also a perennial problem
that some people can 'take it', and others, apparently,
cannot. For it is a true experience that the crucible of suffering purifies and ennobles some characters in such a way that

the person, like Job, seems 'to hear the voice of God in the tempest' and positively radiates peace, joy and life; and others seem to shrink and shrivel and grow daily more bitter.

The Christian facing pain is facing it with Christ. That is easy to say, less easy to live. But it means in the background that this is not just Stoic endurance; it is pain suffered, pain fought, pain accepted, and in a sense pain defeated. The un-understandable element is not removed, but the figure of the suffering Christ somehow penetrates an inner part of us and leads us to greater endurance, in a sense a more living, a more fully human reaction. All the same we are normally left with one or two questionings. Why should *I* suffer? Or why should *they* suffer?

We are sorry, but for us it is useless and time-wasting to discuss this at a reasoning, intellectual level. Certainly we can pursue ideas, but answers are elusive and unsatisfactory. Only by concentrating on God, experiencing him in Christ in yourself, and continuing to live openly and closely to your own pain or to those who suffer does some measure of knowledge come. This cannot really be put in words, but we hope you will come to know what we are getting at in your own facing of pain.

If you truly love God, the pain does not go away, but you live more fully and in a way which can only be experienced. There is a new dimension in which the figure on the cross through pain and death grows glorious, joyous and intensely loving in the resurrection.

Bearing pain

Lord, it is hard for me to understand the saintly Charles de Condren when he said: 'I am most gay when I have most sorrow', as I become gloomy and difficult when I am in pain, and far from joyous. Did he love you much more than I do? I know he regarded the bearing of suffering as a sharing in the redemption of the world with you. Could you help me to love you more so that I may become a channel for you to work through to help heal the distresses of the world? Give me courage and gaiety if my work for you leads to stress and strain and disagreement with others. Make me, in my small way, want to share in the unhappiness and misery of the world. Strengthen me, dear Lord, and stop me from grumbling and complaining.

Lord, the cross has so many meanings, but for me at this moment it is only by looking at you there and letting my pain somehow be joined with yours that I can keep going. I do not know how this happens, but your sufferings make mine bearable and somehow almost understandable. My helplessness is no longer hopeless for you share the burden with me and your silent love brings love into my sufferings. Lord, remain with me in my distress and help me not to fail in comforting others in pain.

In pain and physical distress

Lord Jesus,
You know what pain is like.
You know
    the torture of the scourge upon your back,
    the sting of the thorns upon your brow,
    the agony of the nails in your hands.
You know what I'm going through just now.
Help me
    to bear my pain
    gallantly, cheerfully and patiently,
And help me to remember
    that I will never be tried

above what I am able to bear,
and that you are with me,
even in this valley of the deep dark shadow.
In ev'ry pang that rends the heart,
The Man of Sorrows had a part;
He sympathises with our grief,
And to the suff'rer sends relief.

William Barclay

Use of pain

We ask thee not, O Lord, to rid us of pain; but grant us in thy mercy that our pain may be free from waste, unfretted by rebellion against thy will, unsoiled by thought of ourselves, purified by love of our kind and ennobled by devotion to thy Kingdom, through the merits of thine only Son, our Lord.

Henry S. Nash

Suffering courageously

O God, who hast exhalted the Crucified, the Son, by a triumphant resurrection and ascension into heaven: may his triumphs and glories so shine in the eyes of our hearts and minds, that we may more clearly comprehend his sufferings, and more courageously pass through our own; for his sake who with thee and the Holy Ghost liveth and reigneth, one God, for ever and ever.

Eric Milner-White

For the power to suffer and to triumph

O God,
I don't want anything startling or heroic;

I just want to be able to bear things.
They can do a lot for me,
but sometimes even their drugs don't work.
Help me to bear things
    without grumbling;
    without complaining;
    without whining;
    without self-pity,
        like a good soldier.
Help me
    to pass the breaking point and not break,
You know all about it, Lord Jesus.
You knew
    the mental agony of Gethsemane.
You knew
    the physical pain of the lash,
    of the crown of thorns, of the nails.
I know you won't mind me saying
    that I am glad you went through it all,
    because it means that you can understand
        exactly how I feel.
I know that in the end
    all things pass;
Till then, make me brave,
I wait for your promise of the time
    when there shall be no more pain.
The Psalmist said:
    I kept my faith, even when I said, I am greatly
      afflicted.
    Help me too to keep my faith.

William Barclay

Take me, break me, make me, use me, whatever the pain

When I prayed like this years ago, God, I wanted to
offer you my life. I'm not sure I realised then how seriously

you would take my prayer. It is the breaking part that is so difficult to bear. But then we all need to be moulded by you. Each of us needs the refiner's fire, and sometimes it's pretty hot. If we are to love you and serve you and be happy with you, then some obstacles will have to be overcome, our characters will have to be formed. The rich young man needed to give away all his possessions. That was to be his necessary breaking, and how unhappy he and your Son must have been when he couldn't be broken in this way, couldn't bear the refining. Even your Son, the pioneer of our salvation, we are reminded, was made perfect through suffering.

I know that I shall only be truly happy if I am refined by you and moulded by you so that I can fulfil the purpose for which you gave me life. So I will try to repeat my prayer, more aware of its implications, but more ready to accept the consequences.

Take me, break me, make me, use me.

J.A.I.O.

Pain

I am overwhelmed by pain, and my failure to bear it well; my heart is cold and my mind distracted. I offer all my suffering and failure to you to be united with your Son's cross and passion. I am nothing and have nothing except the pain; do what you want with it and me.

I hurt again, Lord,
I hurt all over.
From the very onset of my sickness I rebelled against pain,
I hid behind my medicine bottles,
I threw myself at you in what must have been pure melo-
drama, begging a reprieve.

Yet somehow you must have seen something valuable about
pain because it is still there.
I suppose I should be thankful, but I'm not very heroic,
I can't smile with gratitude when my body is on the torture
rack.
All I ask, Lord, is that you help me grasp the worth of the
hurt twisting inside me, because if I knew that, maybe I'd
be able to bear up better, maybe then I wouldn't be so
cranky with those I love most.
But no matter what, Lord, just help me to get through
today without being too much of a burden.

Max Pauli

Example of Christ when we suffer

Lord Jesus, who wast silent when men nailed thee to the
cross, and by pain didst triumph over pain, pour the Spirit,
we beseech thee, on thy servants when they suffer, that in
their quietness and courage thou mayest triumph again; who
livest and reignest in the glory of the eternal Trinity, God
world without end.

Daily Prayer

Prayer at the beginning of sickness

Lord, bless all means that are used for my recovery, and
restore me to my health in thy good time; but if otherwise
thou hast appointed for me, thy blessed will be done. O wean
my affection from things below, and fill me with ardent
desires after heaven. Lord, fit me for thyself, and then call
me to those joys unspeakable and full of glory, when thou
pleasest, and that for the sake of thy only Son, Jesus, my
Saviour. Amen.

Thomas Ken (1637-1711)

Sickness

Vouchsafe, good Lord, that as thou hast sent this sickness unto me, so thou wouldest likewise be pleased to send thy Holy Spirit into my heart, whereby this present sickness may be sanctified unto me, that I may use it as thy school, wherein I may learn to know the greatness of my misery and the riches of thy mercy; that I may be so humbled at the one that I despair not of the other; and that I may so renounce all confidence of help in myself, or in any other creature, that I may only put the whole of my salvation in all thy sufficient merits. Amen.

Lewis Bayley (1565-1631)

Pain

Lord, have mercy! What more can I say with this intolerable pain which grips me? I suppose it was like this on the cross?

Your humanity cried out 'Why?'—and I, crucified by pain, join you, Lord.

I offer it for all mankind and particularly those dear to me whose needs I know.

I cannot think or act as I would, but let the bearing of this pain be my prayer.

It cannot go on for ever for either it will get worse and kill me or there will come relief. Lord, thy will be done. Whatever may be—Lord, have mercy.

Colin Stephenson

Lord, why have I to endure this pain? I just can't understand it! I've done everything I think you've asked me to do and lived a good honest life, and now this! Why, Lord? Why me? I can't understand it any more than your servant Job did. I can't understand why you do this sort of thing to the people who try to follow you and keep your commandments. It's not much consolation either to look at what happened to your Son, Jesus. Can't you explain your ways just a little for they seem unfair to me, Lord?

O Lord Jesus Christ, who by thy patience under suffering didst hallow earthly pain and give us an example of thy holy obedience to the Father's will, be near me, I pray thee, in the hours of weakness and pain; sustain me by thy grace that my strength and courage fail not; grant me patience and heal me, if it be thy will; help me to believe that whatever may befall the body is of little moment if thou hold my soul in life, O my Lord and Saviour, who livest and reigneth with the Father, and the Holy Spirit, ever one God, world without end.

Army and Navy Service Book

My strength fails: I feel only weakness, irritation and depression. I am tempted to complain and to despair. What has become of the courage I was so proud of, and which gave me so much self-confidence? As well as my pain I have to bear the shame of my fretful feebleness. Lord, destroy my pride; leave it nothing to feed on. I shall be content if you can teach me by these terrible afflictions that I am nothing, that I can do nothing of myself and that you are all!

François Fénelon (1631-1715)

O my Lord Jesus, I believe, and by thy grace will ever believe and hold, and I know that it is true, and will be true to the end of the world, that nothing great is done without suffering, without humiliation, and that all things are possible by means of it.

O my dear Lord, though I am so very weak that I am not fit to ask thee for suffering as a gift, and have not strength to do so, at least I will beg of thee grace to meet suffering well, when thou in thy love and wisdom dost bring it upon me. Let me bear pain, reproach, disappointment, slander, anxiety, suspense, as thou wouldest have me, O my Jesu, and, as thou by thy own suffering hast taught me, when it comes.

I wish to bear insult meekly, and to return good for evil. I wish to humble myself in all things, and to be silent when I am ill-used, and to be patient when sorrow or pain is prolonged, and all for the love of thee and thy cross.

J. H. Newman (1801-1880)

In illness

I humbly beg of thee, O merciful Father, that this affliction may strengthen my faith, which thou sawest was growing weak; fix my hope which was staggering, quicken my devotion which was languishing, reunite me to my first love which I was forsaking, rekindle my charity which was cooling, revive my zeal which was dying, confirm my obedience which was wavering, recover my patience which was fainting, mortify my pride which was presuming; and perfect my repentance which was daily decaying: for all these and the like infirmities to which my soul is exposed, O make thy affliction my care. Amen.

Thomas Ken (1637-1711)

In pain

Lord, I can't pray much; I am too busy just enduring, just keeping on. You know I want to pray and that my whole being wants to be open to you though I can't do much about it actively. Accept my intention to love you and never let your Spirit cease to pray in the depth of my being.

Short prayers for when in pain

Lord help me!

Support and strengthen me Lord!

Lord, help me to keep going.

My Lord and my God.

Lord Jesus Christ have mercy on me, a sinner.

Lord, I offer all my pain against the terrible pain of the world.

Lord, I offer what I suffer for those who suffer without hope.

If you wish it, Lord, you can save me from suffering or you can cure me. I do not understand why you don't do something but if this is your will, so be it.

You bore the pain of the cross; please help me to bear this agony.

Putting up with minor aches

Lately, Lord,
I've been wondering what cavemen did

when they had a headache,
vitamin deficiency, or iron-poor blood.
Obviously, they didn't run
to their Stone-age medicine cabinets
for some new miracle drug,
so they must have gritted their teeth
and suffered through it unaided.
In this age, that is unbelievable.
If we have a pain, Lord,
we just gulp three green discs
or one red capsule
and we're set for another day.
Yet the medicine show has me worried:
there are too many unknown side-effects
for us to continue throwing pills
recklessly down our throats.
Maybe in the long run,
it's better to endure a minor ache
than to ruin the whole bodily system
with a cure that missed its mark.
Lord, let me remember this
the next time some TV healer
comes on with his pitch.

Max Pauli

Prayer of someone suddenly crippled

O God, it's hell! The pain, the isolation, the lack of real
understanding by so many of my closest friends, feeling
myself a burden, useless, a failure. Heal me. Make me as
physically fit as I used to be. There is so much that I could
do for you with a healthy body.

Your Son, Jesus, at the peak of his career, at the golden
age of thirty-three, could have gone on healing the sick,
making the blind see and the deaf hear, raising the dead,

preaching the good news. But he died because he just had to go on loving, and his outpouring of love killed him. He prayed: 'Let this cup pass from me'. As he continued to pray in Gethsemane the pain and fear did not diminish, but the love welled up and he came to see that in your strength he could bear the suffering. And so he saved the world. When he was most helpless, with hands and feet fixed to the cross, paralysed with pain, he was able to achieve most because he went on loving you and his fellow men, and you gave him strength.

You know what is best for me. Perhaps there are ways in which I shall be able to serve you in a healthy body again and like Job I shall recover. Perhaps I have other gifts which I have neglected because I have been so busy physically. Perhaps I shall be more loving this way. Perhaps . . . Perhaps . . . You know the answers. You are so generous that you will give me strength in whatever way I need it in order to give and receive love. Jesus came to share our lives and to enable us to share his life. His generosity includes Gethsemane. Father, if this cup may not pass, give me strength.

J.A.I.O.

Before going to the doctor

O God,
I can no longer pretend to myself that everything will be
    all right if I just leave things alone.
I can no longer avoid the fact that there is something wrong.
Go with me when I go to my doctor today, and give me
    courage to face the truth about myself.
Make me quite sure that whatever the verdict, I can face it
    with you.
Let me remember the promise of God:
When you pass through the waters I will be with you.

William Barclay

Before going into hospital

Lord, help me, I am dreading going into hospital. There will be no privacy, but people continually about, bustling and noisy. I will never have any peace and quiet in which to pray to you. For even in the night people call out, nurses rush around and talk loudly. Lord, give me a sense of your presence deep within me, and a sense of peace that will persist under all the fuss and bother, for I need your help if I am to remain unflustered and serene.

Before an operation

Jesus, I am very afraid. I do not know what is going to happen to me. I have absolutely no control over what happens and I dislike not being in control. I am afraid of the loss of consciousness that the anaesthetic will bring. I worry that I will be a burden to others after the operation and that I will not be so active again. Lord, help me to trust you. Arrange my life even though it may mean 'my being carried about where I have no wish to go'. (*John 21*.) Let me realise if I die now I will be coming to you whose love casts out fear.

For one to whom strength is slow in coming back

O God,
I'm all right so long as I am lying here in bed, or so long as I
    don't try to do anything; but I have just no strength.
I can't hurry;

I can't even do anything quickly;
I have always to take my time—and it is a long time.
It is so discouraging always to feel weak, and always to feel
    tired.
I want to get back to work, there is so much that I want to
    do, and so much that is waiting to be done.
O God,
give me the patience that I know I must have.
Make me a little better every day until, bit by bit, I can
    shoulder the tasks of life again.
The prophet said:
They who wait for the Lord shall renew their strength.

William Barclay

When I want consolation

O Divine Master, grant that
I may not so much seek
To be consoled, as to console;
Not so much to be understood as
To understand; not so much to be
Loved as to love:
For it is in giving that we receive;
For in pardoning, that we are pardoned;
It is in dying, that we awaken to eternal life.

Attributed to Saint Francis of Assisi (1182-1226)

When feeling dependent and a burden to others

O God, I feel so helpless and such a burden. There is little
that I can do for myself. My friends are so generous with
their time, their strength, their skill. They must have other
things to do. I can't think of any way to repay them. They
are such Good Samaritans.

100

Yes! They are good Samaritans. But let me look more closely at your Son's story of the Good Samaritan. It was provoked by the lawyer's question: 'Who is my neighbour?' when he and Jesus had agreed that the key to eternal life is to love you and our neighbour. Having told the story, Jesus asked: 'Who was neighbour to him who fell among thieves?' 'He who showed pity on him', replied the lawyer. So when I look at the story closely I see it was the neighbour who needed to be loved and the neighbour was the Samaritan, and not the man who fell among thieves. The Samaritan received love by giving it, because that is the way of love. 'Love is something that if you give it away, you end up having more.' It was the sufferer who released the love.

So enable me, Lord, to be truly grateful for the love of my friends, and when I am feeling rebellious and burdensome to remember that if I am humble I can enable them to grow in your love as they give me theirs. Thank you, Lord.

J.A.I.O.

Prayer of a blind, helpless woman

Lord! I thank thee that in thy love thou hast taken from me all earthly riches, and that thou now clothest me and feedest me through the kindness of others.
Lord! I thank thee, that since thou hast taken from me the sight of my eyes, thou servest me now with the eyes of others.
Lord! I thank thee that since thou hast taken away the power of my hands and my heart, thou servest me by the hands and hearts of others. Lord, I pray for them. Reward them for it in thy heavenly love, that they may faithfully serve and please thee till they reach a happy end.

Saint Mechthild of Magdebourg (1212-1280)

Going blind

O God,
It is hard to think of a world
 in which I cannot see the sun and the flowers,
 and the faces of those I love.
It is hard to think of a life
 in which I cannot read or watch things,
  or see lovely things any more.
But even in the dark there will be something left.
I can still have memory,
 and I can still see things again
 with my mind's eye.
I thank you for Braille, which keeps the world of books
 from being altogether closed to me.
I thank you that I will still be able to hear the voices I
 know and to touch the things and people I love.
Lord Jesus you are the Light of Life;
 Be with me in the dark.

          William Barclay

Words of a nun who was told she would lose her sight

 God gave me my eyes: I gave back everything to him when
I entered the order. If he wants my sight, I ask only that I
may see him better.

 Lord I am blind. Please let me see the face of God.

After a stroke

 You've taken away almost everything that I enjoyed,
Lord, and most of me. Please use my uselessness.

Deafness

I used to hear so well and loved what I heard, human voices, music, birds, the sound of trains. Now I'm in a silent world, Lord. People shout at me and grow cross when I don't hear. It embarrasses and hurts me and I cannot now enjoy music or nature or anything with my hearing. I pray I may accept it more and learn to use it.

For cheerfulness in illness

Grant, we beseech thee, almighty God, that we, who in our tribulation are yet of good cheer because of thy loving kindness, may find thee mighty to save from all dangers, through Jesus Christ. Amen.

Roman Breviary

Renewal of health

O God, the source of all health: so fill our hearts with faith in thy love, that with calm expectancy we may make room for thy power to possess us, and gracefully accept thy healing; through Jesus Christ our Lord.

John W. Suter

Heal me, Lord

Lord, I implore you, heal my leg. I can only walk in a lop-sided way and it makes the work I have to do very difficult and sometimes almost impossible as I feel so unsafe and afraid of falling. Lord, you healed so many sick when you were on earth, so why do you not heal me? I don't think I've much less faith than they had. Yet, Lord, if you think it best for me to appear so broken and often to look so afraid, I am content. Heal me deeply, my whole being, and especially my fears and insufficient faith; help me to have greater trust in you and enable me to show forth your wonderful love and joy to those I come in contact with. Heal the whole of me, Lord.

Healing

Lord, there was an occasion in the Gospel when someone called out: 'If it is really your will, make me whole'. And you replied: 'Of course it is! Be whole!' I'm crying out now, Lord. I say if it is your will. Can I take it that it really is? Can I hope and trust? I really mean it, Jesus. Do you?

I lie here day in and day out and watch the world go by. And I feel like the cripple at the pool. Somehow I am never the one selected for healing. But I believe you are the true healer, Lord—sometimes through men and women doctors and others, but sometimes directly. I do not mind how it comes, but Jesus, Son of David, have pity on me. Heal me.

O let the Power fall on I, let the Power fall on I. O let the Power fall on I: let the Power fall on I.

We come together, Lord, to pray for healing. We know each one of us needs to be made whole, to be renewed in your Spirit. And we ask for this. Send your Spirit on us. But we pray most especially and beg your strength and healing hand on *N* and *N* who are sick. Heal them: fill them with life and joy and peace in your love.

Lord, I believe you can cure me, Lord, I trust you can cure me, Lord. Cure me!

She was a faithful believer.
Her sight had almost gone.
She went to a faith-healer, Lord.
There was no change in her condition,
Except that now there was a nagging doubt.
Perhaps she had not enough faith.
Perhaps it was her fault, or maybe you did not really care.
She read the story of the woman with the haemorrhage as a reproach.
Help her, and me, Lord, to see your healing power in the widest terms.
Our disabilities, disadvantages, weaknesses, troubles in life immediately come to mind.
We yearn for their removal.
And yet this is not always to be.
The real miracle of your healing power is the power of salvation, of wholeness, of reconciling a man with yourself.
It is the knowledge that the world has purpose, meaning, and that a man has a place in this, that I have a place in this.
'My daughter, your faith has cured you.'
Her faith and personal encounter with you, Lord, brought wholeness, salvation and the cure was the seal of this.
Remove despair, self-reproach, anger when there is no cure, when we have to continue to live with our disabilities.
Strengthen us for this, by deepening our faith in you.

Rex Chapman

O Lord God, who has spoken by thy apostle, James, saying: 'Is any man sick among you? Let him bring in the

105

priests of the Church, and let them pray over him, anointing him with oil in the name of the Lord, and the prayer of faith shall save the sick man, and the Lord shall raise him up, and, if he be in sins, they shall be forgiven him'; cure, we beseech thee, O our Redeemer, by the grace of the Holy Spirit, the weakness of this sick man (woman), heal his wounds, and forgive his sins, banish from him all pains of body and mind, and mercifully restore him to full health, inwardly and outwardly, that being recovered by the help of thy mercy, he may be able to take up his former tasks. Who with the Father and the Holy Ghost livest and reignest, world without end. Amen.

Rite of Holy Unction

Look down, we beseech thee, O Lord, upon thy servant, failing through bodily weakness, and refresh the soul which thou hast created that, being bettered by thy chastisements, *he* may feel *himself* saved by thy healing. Through Christ our Lord. Amen.

Rite of Holy Unction

The Almighty God, who is a most strong tower to all them that put their trust in him, to whom all things in heaven and earth do bow and obey, be now and ever more thy defence; and make thee know and feel, that there is none other name under heaven given to man, in whom and through whom thou mayest receive health and salvation, but only the name of our Lord Jesus Christ.

Scottish Book of Common Prayer

O God, who by the might of thy command canst drive away from men's bodies all sickness and infirmity; be present in thy goodness with this thy servant that his weakness being banished, and his health restored, he may live to glorify thy holy name, through our Lord Jesus Christ.

Scottish Book of Common Prayer

One whose health is improving

O Lord, whose compassions fail not, and whose mercies are new every morning: we give thee hearty thanks that it hath pleased thee to give, to this our brother, both relief from pain, and hope for renewed health. Continue, we beseech thee, in him, the good work that thou hast begun, that, daily increasing in bodily strength, and humbly rejoicing in thy goodness, he may so order his life and conversation as always to think and do such things as shall please thee through Jesus Christ our Lord.

Church of Ireland Prayer Book

Thanksgiving

Father, we thank you not only for the cures Jesus did, but for what healing people meant to him. We thank you that while so many people thought of disease as inevitable, as a curse of the devil or a punishment for sin, Jesus saw it as the opportunity for showing your love at work. We thank you that when he restored men to health he did so not just as a good thing in itself but as a symbol of something greater still—the breakthrough of your kingdom into human life. Help us to see it that way: to interpret the advances in medical science as symbols of something even greater—as signs of your kingdom in which everything functions healthily, within us, among us, and between us and you. And while men continue to suffer, may we help them to see

how much of this ultimate healing can already be theirs, as
they trust you because of the love revealed in Jesus.

More Contemporary Prayers

Thanksgiving for recovery from illness

O God, great, mighty and revered,
In the abundance of thy loving kindness,
 I come before thee
To render thanks
 For all the benefits thou hast bestowed upon me.
In my distress I called upon thee
 And thou didst answer me;
From my bed of pain I cried unto thee
 And thou didst hear the voice of my supplication.
Thou hast chastened me sore, O Lord,
 But thou didst not give me over unto death.
In thy love and pity
 Thou broughtest up my soul from the grave.
For thine anger is but for a moment;
 Thy favour is for a lifetime;
Weeping may tarry for the night,
 But joy cometh in the morning.
The living,
The living,
He shall praise thee,
 As I do this day,
And my soul that thou didst redeem
 Shall tell thy wonders unto the children of men.
Blessed art thou,
 The faithful physician unto all flesh.

Authorised Daily Jewish Prayer Book

O tender Father, you gave me more, much more even than I thought to ask. It comes to me that our human desires can never really match what you long to give . . . Thanks, and thanks again, O Father, for having granted me what I asked, and that which I neither knew of nor asked.

Saint Catherine of Siena (c. 1347-1386)

Thanksgiving for those who minister to sufferers

O God, I thank you for all who help to overcome or alleviate sickness and suffering. Some of them are known to me and their part is obvious—doctors, nurses, social workers, visitors. Others I never see—research workers, pathologists, makers of surgical aids, drug manufacturers, myriads of administrators. There are so many of them. Now that we have Social Security numbers it must be very easy for them to forget that we are human beings, made in your image because you love us. Now that they are so numerous, and many of them seemingly small cogs in a vast machine, we find it easy to judge and criticise. Help us to see you in one another, and enable those of us who suffer to help those concerned with our well-being by our understanding and prayers.

J.A.I.O.

For those who watch with the sick

Let thy presence, O God, refresh and strengthen all who watch through the night on behalf of others, in sickroom or hospital: that thy peace may continually possess their souls and all anxiety may be lifted from their hearts; through Christ Jesus our Lord.

New Every Morning

MENTAL PAIN AND DISTRESS

Cast your burden on the Lord, and he will sustain you.

Psalm 55.22

The refinement of the torturer who wishes to break a human being goes beyond physical pain and into the realm of the mind. Mental pain or anguish is peculiar to the human being with his power of reasoning and sensitivity at a level differing from the 'bodily senses'. The mind is fed through the senses, seeing, touching, hearing and so on, so what we receive reacts upon the whole person in some degree.

The subtlety of mental pain is that there is no real pain-killer for it except oblivion. We cannot escape from our minds and the attempt to hide in drugs, alcohol, or ceaseless activity is doomed to be eventually destructive of the person.

What belief in God and Christ offers is sometimes seen as another form of drug, an opiate. But we who believe accept that God is fundamentally linked to the human person, psyche–soul–God are intertwined. And so what we offer is not destruction of the person, but an opening-up, a pro-longation, a journey into understanding. For someone suffering from mental pain, understanding, some continued human action, is terribly important. If you are in the midst of it, it often seems that other people are beyond your reach and there is no way out; and if you are a spectator however loving and willing to help, that there is no possible word of hope you can utter.

But it is here especially that prayer, belief, hope, trust, patience and some personal experience of the love of God may carry you through hell or help you to hold together a disintegrating personality.

This is written from personal experience, not from a text book or psychiatric training. It does not suggest refusal of medical or psychiatric treatment, but wants to underline a dimension which can be forgotten, ignored or openly pooh-poohed. The prayers reflect different experiences of the problem. It would be a joy if the attitude was remedial in even one or two instances. We must leave this to you and God.

In times of pain and depression

O God my Father, there are no secrets or problems or mysteries in your sight. Look upon me in my darkness and pain and perplexity. When it is possible, let me sense the touch of your continued compassion and the assurance of your unfailing purpose. Save me from resentment and self-pity, and above all from distrust and despair. Give me grace when I can feel nothing, and see neither plan nor purpose nor ending. Keep me even in the darkness on the right path, and let me never cease to hope for the restoring of light and joy and peace. These things I ask in the name of Jesus Christ your Son and my Saviour.

J.B.P.

O Christ my Lord and Saviour, who knows the frailty of being a human being, and who knows the agony of pain that may come upon mind and body and spirit, look upon me with mercy in my desolation. Forgive me for my failures of faith, my useless longings for the joys of the past and my panic fears for the future. Forgive me for my sins, but save me from the torment of blaming myself for evils which attack but are none of my making.

J.B.P.

When my heart is as cold as stone and I have neither love to give others nor mercy for my own worthlessness, let me know, at least sometimes, that your love for me is changeless and that I must not despisewhat you both love and value. Give something of your own invincible courage, and never let me quench my own flickerings of hope.

J.B.P.

In the certainty of your perfect understanding, even from a bruised and baffled mind I ask for the return of the light and the recovery of joy, and I ask these things in your name.

J.B.P.

O my God, suffer me still—bear with me in spite of my waywardness, perverseness and ingratitude! I improve very slowly, but . . . I protest I will put off this languor and luke-warmness. I will shake myself from this sullenness, and despondency and gloom—I will arouse myself and be cheerful, and walk in thy light. I will have no hope or joy but in thee. Only give me thy grace—meet me with thy grace, I will through thy grace do what I can—and thou shalt perfect it for me. Then I shall have happy days in thy presence.

John Henry Newman (1801-1890)

I am lost. There is nothing but darkness on every side. I am close to despair. Jesu, good Shepherd, take my hand. Please. Please. Please.

I have no longer any control of my thoughts or somehow even of myself. I am overwhelmed by gloom and am in a well of despair, and I cannot lift myself out of it. I suppose I don't even want to, yet I am miserable beyond belief and remaining in it is unending hell. How can you leave me like this, Lord? I cry to you out of the depth of my despair. Give me some glimpse of hope; lift me up out of the depths; send me the kind of help that will penetrate my gloom, for, Lord, I cannot help myself.

Calm my troubled heart; give me peace.
O Lord, calm the waves of this heart; calm its tempests!
Calm thyself, O my soul, so that the divine can act in thee!
Calm thyself, O my soul, so that God is able to repose in thee, so that his peace may cover thee!
    Yes, Father in heaven, often have we found that the world cannot give us peace, but make us feel that thou art able to give peace; let us know the truth of thy promise: that the whole world may not be able to take away thy peace.

Sören Kierkegaard (1813-1855)

On the cross, Lord, they gave you vinegar and gall to kill the pain. Lord, please find a way to kill this ache in my whole being.

Lord, I am distracted; my mind is going in circles. I think I am going mad. Jesus, give me your peace, your deep peace; let it sink into the depth of my being and give me an underlying calmness that will never be disturbed by all the outer distractions and cares of this rushed and busy world, which I find so hard to cope with.

113

Lord, everything is empty and futile and there seems no use in making an effort to keep on. I don't know what to do when this purposelessness engulfs me and drags me down into emptiness. Lord how can you be with me now; you always seem to have known that you were doing your Father's will. Lord, do not leave me in this purposelessness, take away my sense of uselessness; or do you want me to remain this way along with the many who have to live like this nowadays? If you do, somehow or other share the burden of this state and help me to love those who also suffer in this way and who do not have even my faint glimmerings of faith and hope. Strengthen us, dear Lord!

Lord, when this depression comes on me I am weighed down, all joy leaves me, and I am in a state of melancholy gloom that seems unending. There is no way out. No human care or love touches me. I am shut in it. Lord, do not let it come upon me again. If it does, let me know that somehow you are with me in it. Make me realise that you shared this sort of depression on the cross and understand that it's absolute awfulness from which one cannot escape. One is somehow held there in a vice. Lord, be with me, let me know that you love me.

Lord, I am very tense and the slightest thing going wrong makes me want to explode and let fly at people. Lord, you can heal this hurt in me which makes me so taut and brittle and which causes me to blame other people for everything. Say to me: 'peace be still' and help me to let this peace enter into the whole of my being and thaw out my tenseness.

Take me by the hand, Lord, and lift me out of the slough of despond which engulfs me. Without your help and strength I will never get out of it and be able to walk bravely in the world again.

I said:
'Lord, I cannot bear it,
This constant pain—this constant suffering.
Help me—save me—deliver me;
O heal these wounds!'
He said: 'Be still—be calm—listen for my voice'.
I fell into silence,
And in dark waters I waited for him to speak,
to say: 'I will heal these wounds,
I will take them from thee'.
I waited—time stood still.
Then, all at once he spoke;
And oh—he said:
'My heart is wounded too'.

Anonymous (modern)

To the Holy Spirit

What is soiled, make thou pure;
What is wounded work its cure;
    What is parched, fructify;
What is rigid, gently bend;
What is frozen, warmly tend;
    Strengthen what goes erringly.

Anonymous (13th century)

Fear of being rejected

Lord, I am so shut in on myself that even talking to you is hard; but it is much easier than talking to people whom I can see and of whom I'm afraid. Lord, I fear that people will reject me and my small attempts at loving. It is terrible to have love rejected and not to be wanted. I am frightened to take the risk. Jesus, I am told you were rejected by men, so you must know my hopeless feeling, and understand my attempts to protect myself from hurt by seeming indifference and 'couldn't care less' attitudes. Give me love, Lord; help me to break out of myself, but keep me safe too.

Lord, I am dying of jealousy. Help me.

Being hurt by a friend

Lord, sometimes the pain of being hurt by someone whom one loves is less bearable than physical pain which simply numbs. Lord, I have been forgotten by someone whom I love, and though I keep on trying to escape from thinking about it, the thought of it keeps coming back to my mind. Make me remember how your friends deserted you and how you, in love, forgave them. Help me to love more and to forgive however much I am hurt. And Lord, never forget me however often I forget you.

Nameless fears

I do not know why I am afraid or what I am afraid of. I wake in the night with a nameless, faceless panic. I'm empty and in dread. I can't touch it, but it grips me, invades me. Sometimes I lie and hold a crucifix and that helps, Lord, but not always and not altogether. I somehow don't feel it is going away. So in that case let me hold on and live through it. You see, deep down somewhere, I trust you, Lord, and believe. Strengthen this, because, O Lord, the panic . . .

When nervous

What, Lord, shall be my assurance in life; or what comfort of all things under heaven? Surely thyself, my Lord, my God, whose mercies are countless. When was it ever well with me without thee? Or, when was it ill when thou wert by me? . . . It comes to this—there is none I can fully trust to help me in a crisis save thou alone, my God. All seek their own advantage . . . Often a host of friends are not of service to me, nor can the most powerful help me, nor the most shrewd counsel me, nor the writings of the learned comfort me, nor any luxury give me ease, nor the pleasant and secluded place a sense of safety, if thou thyself art not there to teach me and guard me. To thee, then, I look; in thee I trust, my God, the Father of mercies.

Thomas à Kempis (1379-1471)

Fear of being deserted

How can you ever help me, Lord, to get our relationship right again? I lie in bed in the early hours and cannot sleep. It tears at me and I go into a cold sweat of fear that it is all over, that she really will leave, and the one who has my heart will throw it back at me because I am so hopeless with her. I do love her, Lord! Why can't you teach me where I go wrong, and take me by force and change my attitude? I can't bear to think of the alternative—but I can't do any more. So help me God.

Failure

I can't bear to live with the sense of my failure, Lord. Oh, I know I should be humble and accept, and be grateful

to you for life. I'm not, Lord! I twist and turn and scrape
my mind raw with all that might have been—all I wanted
to be and do—and look at me! A failure all round. How
can I stop lashing myself, Lord? I ask you to do something
to me which gets rid of this fearful, destructive self-criticism
—and that lets me live at peace and accept what has happened, so that I can go on from here—not wallow in my
misery.

Desertion

How extraordinary that the Twelve left you like that,
abandoned you in fear, Lord! And you had taught them so
much, loved them so much, been with them so much, and
then—puff—all gone. Didn't it hurt, and how did you so
quickly forgive and forget, and trust them again? I think
you could do so much if you would let us understand
weakness in ourselves and in others, so that we could
understand and accept that we will be let down and let
others down too. Then starting from there may we perhaps
trust each other properly. Amen.

Shame

I am utterly ashamed of the way I behaved and by what
I said. I can't think how it happened; it is terrifying how
awful I can be. I want to hide away from myself and from
others, and forget. But, Lord, I keep remembering, and I
know other people will too. They will think that I am like
this all the time. I find it hard to admit even to you how
stupid I was and how hurtfully I behaved. Please forgive
me and show me how to face other people and get their forgiveness too. Come into my life and rule it in such a way
that I will never behave so badly again. And take my shame
from me.

I've made such a fool of myself—how can I ever go into that company again? They'll all laugh at me, Lord, and poke their fingers at me and sneer. I can't bear it—I hate being a fool—I'm too proud, I suppose. Teach me how you, who were no fool, bore mocking and jeers. Give me humility and courage to go out again, to meet them, and to be able to laugh with them at myself.

When mocked by friends

Lord, the cross you have chosen for me fits perfectly and is excruciatingly painful. You could not have chosen a more self-emptying one. The mocking of people close to me is unbearable. Why did you make me so sensitive? I want to run away and avoid it, to block my ears so I need not hear the criticism, but there is no escape. Other pains I could put up with, but this strips me and exposes all my weaknesses. I am so afraid that in order to get a quiet life I may deny you yet again. I see my weakness and despise it. Strengthen me with your Spirit so I may endure and not run away for, Lord, without you I can do nothing.

Fear

There used to be a phrase, Lord, 'if your knees knock, kneel on them'. Well Lord, mine knock and my belly is like water and I'm sweating with inexpressible fear. So here I am, Lord, kneeling and praying. Come to my aid: quiet my fear: lend me your grace.

Lord, I am afraid. I am consumed with fear; fear that I shall be left alone; fear that I will not have enough money to live on; fear that I shall be attacked in the dark of the night. O Lord, take these fears from me. Help me to remember that you are with me always and because of this I will never be deserted or destroyed for you will hold me up.

119

Lord, if you really care, save me from despair.

Lord, in your mercy, hear my prayer.

Out of the depths have I cried unto you; Lord, hear my prayer.

When I am afraid at night

Lord, when I am afraid of sleep and afraid of the darkness, make me remember that in peace I can lay me down in sleep, for you alone make me to dwell in safety, and that the darkness is not dark to you. Lord, help me to put my trust in you when I am afraid.

Strengthening

Lord, your servant Paul said: 'When I am weak, then am I strong'. I feel so weak, pray God I may be strong.

Lord, I call on you as the almighty. You can do all things. Give me strength against my temptation to despair.

The joy of suffering

O my God, my God, unhappy and tormented was my childhood, full of torments my youth. I have lamented, I have sighed, and I have wept. Yet I thank thee, not as the wise Sovereign; no, no, I thank thee, the one who art infinite love for having acted thus! Man has before him a life of thirty, forty, perhaps seventy years; in thy love thou hast prevented me from buying for this sum just the little sweets of the kind for which I would have no memory in eternity,

120

or which I would even recall for my eternal torment—as having bought the worthless.

Thou hast obliged me (and there were also many moments in which thou hast spoken with kindness but of the same thing, not that I should escape the suffering but that it was even thy love that placed me in these sufferings). Thou hast obliged me to buy these sufferings: blessed. For each suffering thus bought is the communion in suffering with thee, and is for ever and forever an eternal acquisition, for one remembers only one's sufferings.

Sören Kierkegaard (1813-1855)

A mentally handicapped child

We love him so much, Lord. In a way he is the centre of the family. Yet we have to ask why is he like this, Lord? We have to ask what do you want of him and of us? How can we live so that all the children gain and he gains, and no one, even us, loses? When we sit together sometimes we are just empty as we look at him. We fear the future for him when we are gone, for the world is unkind to such as him. We go on questioning and suffering, but in a way the main suffering is that we love him so much, Lord, and will what is best for him, even when it seems too much for us.

We pray now together, Lord, because we are man and wife, and he is the flesh of our flesh. He came into this world because we loved each other and we wanted him so much. But, honestly, we did not want him like this. He was to be our pride and joy as we watched and helped him to grow. How could either of us want him to be like this? And yet, you allowed this to happen. Can't you see we must ask questions? Can't you see, as our Father, that we human parents could not want this for our son? How can you per-

121

suade us that this is the way, your way, the loving way? Honestly it isn't our way! But we want so much for him and we know we don't know all the answers. So we ask your help, for us to understand, for us to keep faith and hope and love; for us to love him and care for him as he needs love and care, not for our selfish selves. And for him, Lord, well just that he may be happy, and that people will love him and be kind to him, and yes, Lord, that he may know you and feel your love. It's so hard to believe, so hard to trust, so hard to love, give us strength.

Despair at change

Lord, I am in despair. Life as I have known it is crumbling into ruins. I have been looking for human support and have found none. My friends are too busy, probably with things and people of much more importance than I. And, Lord, you do not seem to be giving me much help either. If you are good, please give me some light in the great darkness which surrounds me, and give me strength to bear my burdens which are too great for me alone.

Christian sadness

Yet Christian sadness is divine
    Even as thy patient sadness was:
The salt tears in our life's dark wine
    Fell in it from the saving cross.

Bitter the bread of our repast;
    Yet doth a sweet the bitter leaven;
Our sorrow is the shadow cast
    Around it by the light of heaven.

O light in Light, shine down from heaven.

Francis Thompson (1859-1907)

THE LONELY, THE DEPRIVED, THE DESERTED

He was despised and rejected of men.

Isaiah 53.3

There is something written somewhere to the effect that 'loneliness is the price of individuality'. Well, yes, it probably is, but don't most of us get torn between wanting to be alone (or at least not bossed about, made into a number, de-personalised) and yet wanting to be with, to be part of?

It is a terrible thing for a naturally 'clubbable' person to be deserted by a husband, a wife, a friend: it is even more awful, probably, for someone who has never known what it is to be 'part of'.

There are all sorts of modern conditions which lead to 'cut-off-ness', divorce, social ostracising, mental barriers, snobbery, personal insecurity. Some of these individual problems we feel, some are part of the human lot, some we can see working out (often bitterly) in others.

Sadly, one emphasised characteristic of the present age is the running away from self-loneliness and reality which is often superficially present among drug-takers, over-heavy drinkers and some psychological cases. Normally to run away is to undermine one's human possibilities, to be less than a man. Sadly too (those who are on the border-line know this) some long not to run away, and suffer untold misery because they do run away.

These prayers inadequately cover some of these situations, as we have received prayers or as we have personally experienced or tried to articulate the almost unspoken prayers of those alongside whom we have lived in many a crisis.

There is real agony, desperation or despair in individuals at these times or in these circumstances. Not infrequently they are themselves almost untouchable, unreachable in their very isolation.

123

But they both need to contact and to be contacted. It is a deeply Christian characteristic to be sensitive to people in these needs—'When I was in prison you visited me'. And it can be of real value for a deserted person, through the medium of prayer, to break back into near-human relationships.

Particularly in the case of drug-takers and those branded as criminals, the outstanding need is strong underlying hope.

O God help me to remember when I feel lonely, deserted or unloved that neither death nor life, nor angels, nor principalities, nor powers, nor things present, nor things to come, nor heights, nor depths, nor any other creature, not even myself, is able to separate me from your love which is in Christ Jesus our Lord.

Adapted from Romans 8.38-39

Loneliness

Lord, the night is lonely,
> the darkness wraps us, each in his own world,
>> and no night is more lonely, or darkness deeper,
>> than Gethsemane's night:
>> the others do not understand their world is dark
>>> only because their eyes are closed in sleep.
>> You tried to explain, Lord,
>>> as you knelt and washed their feet,
>>> speaking of service,
>>> as you broke bread, passed the crumbling
>>> pieces from hand to hand,
>>> speaking of a body broken,
>>> as you handed them a cup, speaking of

a new covenant, sealed in your blood;
water, bread, wine, washing, body, blood, vine,
Comforter, love, life, death, life
—they blinked their bewilderment;
in three days they shall begin to understand,
but not yet; now, they have fallen asleep.
Lord, we are sometimes lonely because we cannot make
ourselves understood;
there is nothing more personal than fear,
locked up inside us,
a feeling without any rational explanation.
Others may sleep peacefully in Gethsemane,
but we see the trees in the moonlight, their
contorted branches frozen in the mad
dance of death:
trees, how could the others understand what
our fears have made of them?
Loneliness robs us of language, and others of
understanding.
Look, Lord, at these lonely ones,
a woman, basket in hand (enough food for one),
returning from the shops where she has spoken
to another human being for the first time
since yesterday and for the last time until
tomorrow, unlocks her door and reluctantly
shuts it, nobody to be shut out, only herself
to be shut in:
a man, on hospital bed, the family visited
yesterday evening, and now he awaits the
theatre-trolley,
to be carried into anaesthetised oblivion,
and none can enter with him;
a minister, remembering his call, the fire that
burned in his belly and tempered his heart,
going to meet a regiment of empty pews,
to worship in a museum of Victorian
nonconformity, to break bread with the

dwindling few, looking for the resurrection . . .
Lord, hear the prayer you uttered for them, watch with them
this hour and the next.

Michael Walker

Lord no one cares what happens to me. It is awful not to
be wanted, not to be noticed by my neighbours, not to have
anyone to talk to. Help me, Lord; let me meet someone
who will care and who will take an interest; someone who
will listen to me and not simply as a duty. I know you listen
but I don't seem to hear your replies. Fill the emptiness of
my life. Stop me from becoming embittered by the prospect
of long, empty, loveless days. Find me a friend and help
me to know you as a friend.

I'm desperately lonely, Lord. Even though I live in a city
and in a crowd, though I'm with people all day and everyone thinks I have lots of friends, deep inside I'm lonely,
Lord. I've never really found anyone I could talk to like
I'm talking to you. No one seems to want to know. They
are so full of their own problems. They don't really want
mine. Teach me about aloneness, Jesus, because you must
have been alone too. How do I live with myself, Lord?
Tell me.

Lord, I do not want to be alone. I have not chosen it.
I know that there are those who lead a solitary life and are
happy because it is what they have desired; but I am by
myself because no one has asked me to go anywhere and I
suppose it is because they find me dull and unattractive.
It is you who made me, Lord, and so you must love me
and I know you value me because you would have died
upon the cross if I had been the only soul to save.

I can speak to you and I do not bore you. Wherever I go you are my companion and there are few of the heedless crowd which push me aside who know that I carry you in my heart.

Lord, I am not worthy to have you under my roof, but thank you for coming, for without you I should be nothing.

Having you I carry the whole universe, for you are everything and I live in you.

This is what I have to share, for to keep this richness for myself alone would be a denial of your love. Already I feel the urge to find another lonely person and to be the means of awakening them to your presence, for you live in me.

Colin Stephenson

I feel so isolated from everyone, Lord,
the way Adam felt in the garden before you gave him Eve.
ISOLATED . . .
the word sounds like an iceberg lost in an infinite ocean of
    silence.
I know I shouldn't feel this way,
that I have many friends only a phone call away,
that you at least are here.
But I still feel it gnawing at me.
This dark mood will pass—
it always does—
but right now I'm trapped in it,
so I might as well put it to use.
After all,
it's probably just your way of letting me know
how dependent I am on others who support me,
how without them I am less than nothing.
All right, Lord,
I thank you for this insight, but now,
please help me to stop feeling blue.

Max Pauli

Nobody cares

This week I have not spoken to anyone, Lord, and no one has spoken to me. I've been out in the street, but they all passed by so busily: no one smiled and said 'good morning' —no one cares. I might just as well be a ghost, not there at all. Now I am back in my room. There are sounds of life around me, Lord, traffic in the street, someone's transistor, there is even the smell of someone's supper. O Lord, I'm so lonely; I'm just sitting here wanting to die. No, not really— wanting someone to care, someone to love me, someone just to come in and say 'hello'. Send someone, Lord, or teach me how to live alone with you.

A prayer when lonely

Lord, I am lonely but I will try to remember when you hung upon the cross and had given your beloved mother to the care of your apostle John, you accepted 'the loneliness of the world since time began'.

I will try to remember too the love you poured into the world by that loneliness and by dying on that cross for me that I might have life eternal.

And in remembering and seeing more clearly the depth of your love may I offer my loneliness for those who have forgotten and fill the world with pain.

Rosa George

Show me how to approach my sense of being alone and cut off so that it may not any longer be a condition to be dreaded, but rather seen as a means to closer dependence on you. Let my soul learn in solitude the lesson of your presence.

A Book of Private Prayer

Lord, there was another hillside, where once you spoke of
    God's care for all that he had made:
    You stooped and picked a wild flower—the pageantry
    of Solomon's court was tawdry compared to the care
    and artistry God had lavished on this, you said;
    as birds wheeled in flight above the crowds, shrill
    song, swift descent, God feeds them, you said;
    and you looked at the men, women and children around
    you—the hairs on your head are counted, God knows
    you all, you said.
Lord, this is not that hillside, no pilgrims temple-bound
    come here,
    no children know this place, only ghouls who can
    watch another man's pain;
    no flowers grow amidst these rocks, the fallen seed
      is snatched away, or dies in the sun;
    birds of song are banished, this is the territory of
      vultures;
    here the hairs on a man's head, his limbs, his flesh,
      his mind, his senses are as nothing, human life
      is cheap.
Where is now your God?
Lord Jesus, that cry from the cross makes us tremble: and
    fills us with hope.
    We know that place where God is, his presence
      felt, his Spirit known;
    we know too that place where it seems that God
      is not, the abyss into which we plunge
      either by our own treachery or the cruel
      circumstance that throws us down into darkness;
    the abyss, Lord, Lord Jesus, Holy Son of God the
      Father, you know it too, deeper than
      any depths we can imagine, a darkness beyond
      our conceiving, the darkness of God's absence
      into which he enters for whom God is all

and in all.
And now, Lord, everywhere, even where it seems
    that God is not, you are there.
If I make my bed in hell, you are there also.
How often in this generation, Lord, has your cry been
    wrung from men's lips. We remember them, those
    who felt forsaken by God:
        the Jewish child, naked, shorn head, torn from
        parents, choking gas in the terrible death of
        Auschwitz;
        the family, father, mother, children, huddled in
        their home as bullets rake the street of their
        Vietnamese village:
        a man who watches cancer invade the body of a
        loved one, and sees pain that knows no
        pity destroy without haste;
        the black man bearing insult, 'Nigger!' from
        loose lips, 'Coloureds need not apply' from
        advertisement column.
Lord, their cry is your cry:
        you have been where they are,
        there is no going beyond your presence.
We pray that you will give to them the grace of Calvary:
        the grace which, having endured the moment
        when God is no more, finds that God is all.

Michael Walker

Deprived

I've never had a proper home, Lord, always shifted about
living in other people's houses. You had nowhere to lay
your head, so you know what it is like, Jesus Christ, but I
don't think I'm as tough as you. Lord, give me somewhere
that I can call home.

Approved school

They are so young, Lord, to be classed as needing special care, unfit for general society. Oh, I know I don't have to cope with any one of them in a family and I'd probably be no better than any other parent if faced with such a problem kid. But that's not the point really, Lord. I want you to help them. I want you somehow to break the chain which leads from approved school to borstal to prison. Break it, Lord. Set them on their feet, draw them into society and into family: let them open up to love and respond to love and grow in every way to the full stature of men and women. For their sakes and for ours, keep them free from crime.

Borstal boy

It seems such a waste of youth and vigour and all that might be, when I live with these young lads in borstal. You know, Lord, I sometimes begin to know a little what you mean by the sins of the fathers working out in their children. So many come from broken homes; what chance have they ever had? Is it fair, Lord? Can I ever hope they will get the chip off their shoulders, work and play, marry and escape from their crippling past. This I pray, Lord, let them grow into real manhood. Let them love and let them care and let them respect themselves and let them know joy.

In prison

You tell me to love all men, my brothers, Lord. How can I do that in here? Most of the time I'm not really treated as a man, and the others are out for what they can get. There is no love here, Lord. I'm cut off from it at home, and letters and visits aren't the same. Oh Lord, there is no love here. How can I love all men my brothers?

I'm not a person; I'm a thing, Lord. I'm a number and a case and a crime. Lord, let me be a person again, let me not lose myself or get bitter. Lord, let me be!

Banging up, banging up! O Lord, will they never stop banging up!

O Lord, how can I even hope to listen to the chaplain when he talks of God's love and the compassion of Jesus in this bedlam of bluster and brutality; help me, at least, to keep a picture in my mind, if not in my cell, of Christ at the scourging pillar.

M. P. Grace

I don't know if she is going to wait, Lord. I love her very much and she has stood by me till now. But can she wait those years, Lord? I can, I've got to, but will she? My mind goes round and round in fear and questioning. O Lord, let her wait, make her wait. I love her so, and I need her so. Please, Lord, make her wait!

I didn't think it could really ever happen—that I'd end up inside. That nightmare of arrest, of police van, of police station and accusation. The sick, dreary, empty, hopeless feeling, the 'no way out', and the 'if only I hadn't done it', the panorama of 'might-have-beens' chasing the panorama of 'never-will-be-now'. Oh Lord, the awful, empty, desperate me. Help me through. I don't deserve your help; I've thrown sonship in your face. But Lord, when no one else loves me or cares, do not drop me too. Love me, Lord.

But, Lord I don't feel guilty, I haven't got remorse; I still think that there are people outside who should be in my place in prison. Come, and be near me and whisper, perhaps, to me 'would you crucify me again, then?'

M. P. Grace

Under unjust sentence

Lord, I am full of bitterness; there is no prayer in me— only curses for the malice and stupidity of men—could you accept my bitterness and maybe change it? Perhaps turn it into acceptance—or forgetfulness through some way of your own. I can't.

M. P. Grace

Lord, that judge was really getting at me; perhaps he had a row with his wife that morning; but he did slap me down. Six months for a daft thing like that! How can I not rebel. O Lord, throw me your cross, sling your crown of thorns at me—anything to make me stand in your place for even a minute.

M. P. Grace

Prayer of a life-sentenced murderer

Dear Lord, life for me since early childhood has been a hard struggle. I suffered acutely during my childhood, having no mother or father to love or care for me.

At that age I didn't know much about life, only that I was sick of it. Upon leaving school, Lord, my whole being rebelled at orthodox authority and undue restraint. I was

133

overpowered with hatred and frustration. Dreading ridicule and wanting to be 'with it', I said many unkind things about you, Lord. It was not until I started this prison sentence that I searched for you, Lord. Should I have waited until the chips were down before starting my search? Perhaps not, Lord. What I do know is that my life of imprisonment has become one of freedom. I have a feeling of strength and happiness; prison is only a physical constraint.

It has not been easy, Lord. At first I wanted to tear the veil that seemed to hide you, only to fall back on myself. I still fail many times, but joyfully rise with new strength. Sorrows and troubles are all around me still, but I no longer feel them in the same way; they have lost their power to wound.

Lord, it is a hard road ahead with a myriad paths leading to destruction, and my prayer is that when I chance to step along one such path, you, Lord, will never tire of loving and caring, and bringing your sheep back to the road of salvation. Amen.

J.W.

Prayer of a prison warder

Lord, help me to realise that in spite of what men say, I have a vocation; even in a 'screw's' uniform I can bring Christ to poor criminals; by making an effort to be compassionate, not to condemn or despise. Oh, I know they'll con me and make a monkey out of me; but let it all come and then, I'm sure you'll take a few steps nearer me.

M. P. Grace

Prisoners of war and political captives

Lord, you know how lonely I feel here. There is only you, when I can reach you, and the one or two precious friends on whom I can rely. Help me so to support them and them to support me that together we may uplift your cross and your healing gospel in this place.

Lord, help me to control the chaos of my mind in this state of humiliation. Teach me to concentrate my thoughts on wholesome objectives and kindly, helpful thoughts for other people, both warders and fellow prisoners. Show me how to extract satisfaction from the simple things of daily routine and in what I find around me. Let me draw some good for the future out of even the most unlikely circumstances, while trying always to set an example for good. When I hope to sleep at the end of the day, may I see your face.

Lord, when will it end and I be free again? Make me submit to your will and be grateful for the tiny pleasures and small satisfactions which come my way. Fill me with love of you and of my fellow prisoners and guards, even the most morose and bestial, for they need it most. Release me when you ultimately please, but release me, if it is your will, richer and not poorer in spirit from my experiences here.

George Guthrie Moir

Drugs

I get all confused about your creation and what we do with it. Take drugs, Lord. They can do such wonderful things in medicine, like killing pain or healing disease. And then look at them and their other uses: the person who can't sleep without them, the heroin addict who is killing himself by his doses, the young people who go on trips and somehow don't quite come back the same. Lord, help us all to be whole and to know and love and serve without having to resort all the time to drugs. And where someone is hooked, show us how to help them off that hook and into a fuller life. Amen.

135

He comes in smashed, Lord, at any time of night. He knows he is running away, but he says he cannot relate to people and that he takes pills so that he can feel with them more. Then somehow he doesn't really feel that and he gets so depressed that I could weep for him and he sometimes does for himself. What can I do, Lord? I'm here and I try to be friendly and loving, to be patient and kind. For a time it seems to work and then he goes off again. He's so weak and he knows he is. Lord, please give him strength. Let him love himself instead of despising himself, give him purpose, open him up, let him find himself and be a man.

Drug addict

I don't know if I want to talk to you, God: why should I? You seem to have made me so that I cannot relate to anyone so why should I try to relate to you? Yet I need someone, God. Are you there? Do you care? No one else does! At least I get warmth when I'm high, I lose my shyness and I become a person. Oh God, it doesn't last and then I'm down again and I just wait until I can get smashed again. Oh God, Oh God, Oh God, I love it and I hate it and what am I to do?

There is something about the needle, Lord. Oh, in cold soberness, it sounds horrid, but it gets me, Lord. It's like a great longing, a hunger, and I know I'll be after it again. It gives me a kick and gets me into people. Then part of me hates me and despises me for it. It is like an evil sickness when I think like that, and then I'm at it again. Oh Lord, strengthen me. I'm so weak and it's so subtle and strong. Strengthen me, Lord.

Daughter on drugs

I can't bear to see her, Lord, that lovely daughter of mine. She's listless and drowsy, she doesn't wash now and her hair is a mess. Tell me how I can help, Lord. What does she need, what is lacking in us that this has happened? Where do we turn now? Please keep her father from getting at her. I don't think that's the way, but what is the way, Lord? I know you are the way, and that's why I'm asking, but for us and for her Lord? She is cut off from us. What is her way, Lord?

Drugs

They say you've gone to heaven,
But I have heard them tell
That before you went to heaven, Lord,
You also went to hell.
So come down, Lord, from your heaven,
For if you went to hell,
Come down into the clip joint, Lord,
Come down to us as well.

Smoke rises in your churches
To praise your holiness.
Smoke rises from our reefers
To cloud our loneliness.
So come down, Lord, from your heaven,
To call, to heal, to bless.
You know that our smoke-rings
Are signals of distress.

The sick they need a doctor
More than the healthy do.
They say you took a dying thief
To Paradise with you.
So come down, Lord, from your heaven.
If what they say is true,
Come down into this den of thieves—
There's thieves have need of you.

They say you were victorious
Over hell and over death.
We know the hell of heroin,
The dying that is meth.
So come down, Lord, from your heaven,
You whom we can't confess,
And be the resurrection
Of this, our living death.

Kenneth Leech

Alcohol

Lord, he's at the bottle again. It is so sad to see because he is ruining himself and he is not really happy. And the awful thing is he's ruining our love, Lord. How can I love him when he is so full of drink that he shouts and swears and even hits me? It is separating us, Lord, and hard as I try it makes me sick and full of fear when he comes in like that. Lord, let him see what it is doing to him, before it is too late, and give me the courage to hold on and see him through. I love him, O Lord, but stop his drinking.

Homosexuals

He is so lonely, Lord. His emptiness and the lack of anyone to love drive him to degrade himself by wandering the streets and public places trying to pick someone up. I really don't know what I can do for him, Lord, or what I can ask for him. He is yours and you promised the fulness of joy. But this seems barred to him, Lord, and I fear that despair will creep up on him and lead him to something desperate, and even to suicide. I don't think doctors can help very much, and I know I can't so really it's up to you, Lord. I'll promise to do my best, and to be about, but only you can help. Please do!

She is sweet, Lord, and beautiful too. I never could think why she wasn't getting married. Then one day she told me, in floods of tears, in hate of herself and in near despair. She could only feel real attraction towards and love for her own sex, she said, and then she burst again. Oh Lord, how can you let this happen to a girl? It's your fault, you know, Lord, because she is yours. Can't you do something now? Can't she learn to love a man? She so truly longs to, and tries so hard; she wants to marry, but she doesn't dare. She is afraid, Lord. So, please give me the patience to listen, to help her if I can, the strength and love to give her hope. And will you give her the courage to go on and the chance to break through into a new love? Amen.

Lord, I love him very much. You know I am engaged to him and we are supposed to be getting married soon. But now he's told me, Lord. He says he's a homosexual, but still loves me, and I love him. Can we, should we give up now? Must we break up? Would I be loving and strong enough to go on, knowing this? Will our real love for each other carry us through? There are so many questions and so few answers that mean anything. It was such an awful shock. But I love you and I love him, and he says he still loves me; so what are we to do, what are we to do?

I ask only to be accepted, Lord, and not despised or turned out. I am what I am; there seems no other way. But in praying for this, I want to add, Lord, don't let me hurt anyone else, but only love them and allow them to grow into fulness.

The Agony of Civil Strife

'What was the pain I suffered, Johnny, bringin' you into the world to carry you to your cradle, to the pains I'll suffer carryin' you out o' the world to bring you to your grave!

139

Mother o' God, have pity on us all! Blessed Virgin, where were you when me darlin' son was riddled with bullets, when me darlin' son was riddled with bullets? Sacred Heart of Jesus, take away our hearts o' stone and give us hearts o' flesh! Take away this murdherin' hate, and give us thine own eternal love.'

From 'Juno and the Paycock' by Sean O'Casey

Pain of violence

Lord, I am bewildered by the evil and violence in the world today. I passionately want to fight it; I would like to shoot the terrorists that kill hostages, the snipers that kill innocent people. Then suddenly I see the power of evil is breeding violence in me. Lord, it is terrifying! Keep before my eyes the example of Jesus who confronted evil not with violence but with goodness. Teach me the way of love which will let your power into the world and stop me from wanting to be violent for this will be only increasing violence. Show me how to bring love into my daily life, even if it leads to my having to suffer much; also give me faith, and hope for the future of mankind.

Evil in the world

Lord, the world seems to be torn by evil. People fight each other for money, material goods, for ideals, for social justice, in a bitter way, and they cease even to try to respect each other. Lord, make us look at each other without prejudice; teach us to see each person as an individual and not as 'the enemy'. Work through us so we can love others as your children and make others loving to us too, for only with the help of your redemptive love can the forces of hate and destruction be overcome.

The power of evil

Lord, I do not understand why man can do such evil things. Ordinary men become violent, beat up the helpless, knife each other. Lord, we, who think ourselves so clever, so rational, hide from ourselves that there is a powerful force of evil ever ready to work in man and to take possession of him. We like to laugh at the idea of the devil as a creation of simpler civilisations. Help us to perceive the strength of the power of evil which can so easily take control of us if we forget you, and fail to call on you for strength, and for your Spirit to make us loving rather than hating. Deliver us from evil, Lord.

The cosh comes in, when the cross goes out.

Wayside Pulpit

Lord God,
you want the well-being of men
and not their destruction.
Take all violence from our midst,
Extinguish hatred in our hearts,
Curb the passion in us
that makes us seek each other's lives.
Give peace on earth
to all mankind.
We ask you this
through Jesus Christ, our Lord.

Huub Oosterhuis

My skin is different

They said that this world was developing at a rapid pace,
making ingenious scientific achievements.
Yet, instead of giving me a helping hand to go forward,
I'm being pushed back and degraded,

141

because of my brown skin.
I'm being told that I will only be employed
as a nanny or shop-girl.
Is this what they call 'ingenious progress'?
I don't see the difference between now
and fifty years ago, Lord. Is there one?

We sometimes feel inclined to say:
'Why did I have to be born brown?'
It's a question that comes so naturally to all of us.
But I'm happy to be your creation, Lord,
your unique individual thought.
I was the creation of my parents too,
because they loved each other.
Aren't they entitled to the love
you talked about, Lord?
Whether it be in the form of a black or white child,
does it matter, as long as it's your idea.
Or must they refrain from living and loving,
because they do not belong to a white society?

Where do I go from here, Lord?
The whites don't want me.
I'm just the result of 'some stupid ancestor of theirs who
couldn't keep his hands off an African woman'.
I don't fit into the black ghetto either.
They're resentful, because I'm a little lighter than they are,
and I speak the white man's language.
I don't belong with them.
Where do I belong, Lord?
Will you help me search for my identity?
I'm not black and I'm not white—
I'm in between.
I'm on neither side, and yet on both sides.

I can hear your voice now, Lord—
it's rather soft and inaudible,

but it seems to be saying:
'You're the missing link, my beloved child.
We've waited a long time,
and now at last you can close the drift
and link the opposing ghettos.
Why do you think I've made you like that—
in colour, in feeling . . .
You are passionate and you want to be free
to live, to live my life.
It's taken a long time, my child,
but at last you're beginning to see
that you belong to neither race,
yet you are part of both.
It is you who must bring unity.'

'Lord, make me truly human': teenagers' prayers from
Salisbury, Rhodesia

Pain of growing old

I hate all this giving up, Lord. I used to be young and strong and now I'm getting older and can do less. I know this is bound to be so but I hate it. I get jealous of young people, cross that I can't read without glasses, annoyed when I can't hear, hurt when I am ignored. And I know it will be worse and life will perhaps be lonelier and emptier! Now I don't want just to grumble, Lord, because there is a lot of love about and care and kindness. But I even hate people being kind to me. How silly can I be? Will you help me to be more patient and loving?

Pain of old age

Lord Jesus, it is hard to go on living now I am so old and so many of my friends have died. People do not really want

143

me; I am a burden to others as I cannot look after myself. I would like so much to come to you and know you face to face. Why do you keep me here? Often it is very hard to understand why; then I remember your most loved and most loving disciple, John, who lived to be nearly a hundred, suffered a more terrible martyrdom than the other disciples, that of not being able to lay his life down for you, of having to live many lonely years without the sight of you when he had known you so well in the flesh. John's pain must have been so much greater than mine, but for love of you he did not complain, but wrote of you and, no doubt, told others about you. Help me to do this too in my small way. May my loving adoration help others to love you more!

SPIRITUAL DESOLATION

My God, my God, why hast thou forsaken me?

Mark 15.34

This sounds a grandiose term which we might be tempted to say would never fit us. But it expresses a reality which humanly appears an absurd paradox. Quite simply this state very often engulfs a person who has been used to praying, to serving God, to believing deeply.

Slowly or suddenly, as the case may be, there is no longer sureness of belief; prayer is dry, empty, tasteless; any approach to God is an effort! There is a feeling of 'What's the use? Why bother! I couldn't care less.'

This can happen to anyone, whether they are trying to pray or not. Perhaps at some stage of life it happens to most people, so what we need to do is to understand it a little and then openly to live through it, with will, more than feeling. Because . . . long though the state may last, and by long we mean not days but weeks, months or years sometimes, there is normally a lightening of gloom, an end to the tunnel.

Perhaps the first important lesson to learn is that this is a common state and one used by God, but each of us needs to react to it rightly. If we simply drift, we simply drift! God does not usually take us up, like Habbakuk, by the hair of our head. We are human beings with minds and wills of our own and he wants us to use them.

Often then it is a matter of living through the period, but in a positive way; making acts of faith, living positively by faith, praying 'out of the depth', hoping.

From God's point of view, it seems to be an important element in our growth that we have this greyness, that we are emptied. that we learn to persevere the hard way!

In this state we must trust and keep on trying. In this

condition not much is of help, but sometimes a person who is in it or has gone through it can give a word of encouragement which makes the grey less grey, the dryness less dry.

My God, my God

Often I moan and groan because you seem so far away, so quiet and uninterested. I even say, perhaps you're dead or don't exist. But what a fantastic idea—you, Christ, are God and man. As you begin to lose your manhood in the death agony, you lose God too. Lose God—is it possible? I can't conceive it, but suppose it is so—God's sense of God is blotted out. What a terrible and incredible thought. As though it was the end of God, a nothingness, a gnawing emptiness, all being gone, poured out, spent. Good God, I must try to be in that and feel what it is like as man, and then remember that you were God. Oh God!

I thought loving you would be only joy, Lord. Why this pain, this darkness?

Lord, my darkness, my desolation, my depression is weighing me down. I am at breaking point; it is horrible, messy, grey, cold, and empty. Why have you left me in this? Why are you not with me now when I need you? People tell me I am suffering this for others who have never known you. I just don't believe it at this moment. Get me out of this, be with me, let me know that you are with me.

Jesus prays to the Father that the cup may pass from him, and his Father hears his prayer; for the cup of suffering will indeed pass from him—but only by his drinking it. That is the assurance he receives as he kneels the second time in the garden of Gethsemane that suffering will indeed pass as he accepts it. The cross is his triumph over suffering.

Suffering means being cut off from God. Therefore those who live in communion with him cannot really suffer. This Old Testament doctrine was expressly reaffirmed by Jesus. This is why he takes upon himself the suffering of the whole world, and in doing so proves victorious over it. He bears the whole burden of man's separation from God, and in the very act of drinking the cup he causes it to pass over him. He sets out to overcome the suffering of the world, and so he must drink it to the dregs. Hence, while it is still true that suffering means being cut off from God, yet within the fellowship of Christ's suffering, suffering is overcome by suffering, and becomes the way to communion with God.

Suffering must be endured in order that it may pass away.

Dietrich Bonhoeffer (1906-1945)

There is no penance more bitter than this state of pure faith without sensible support: whence I conclude that it is the penance the most real, the most crucifying, and the most exempt from all illusion. Strange temptation! We impatiently seek for sensible comfort out of fear of not being sufficiently penitent! Ah, why don't we practise for penance the re-nouncing of that consolation, which we are so tempted to seek after? In fine, we must call to mind Jesus Christ, whom his Father abandoned upon the cross: God withdrew all comfortable sentiment and reflection, that he might hide himself from Jesus Christ: this was the finishing stroke of the hand of God, which smote that man of sorrows: this was what consummated the sacrifice. We must never abandon ourselves more to God, than when he seems to forsake us. Let us receive therefore the light and the comfort when he sheds it upon us, but without attaching ourselves to it: When he plunges us in the night of pure faith, let us readily enter into that darkness, where all is agony.

One moment in this tribulation is worth a thousand: we are troubled, and we are in peace: God not only hides himself from us, but he hides us also from ourselves, to the end that all may be in faith. We feel ourselves discouraged, and yet we have an immovable will that wills every severity which God wills: we will everything, we accept everything, even the trouble by which we are tried: thus we are secretly in peace by the means of this will, which is preserved in the centre of the soul for enduring the conflict. Blessed be God who doth such great things in us, notwithstanding our unworthiness.

François Fénelon (1631-1715)

When prayer is dark

Lord, prayer is dark and I cannot think at all. I know you can only be reached by love and not by the mind, but, Lord, my love seems dead and without feeling. I know nothing at all except that I want to love you and cannot. Give me courage to endure the darkness and faith to believe that you are with me in this emptiness.

Desolation

Lord, I know that you told your disciples that it was necessary for you to go away and leave them, and that this emptiness, this dryness which I am experiencing now must be like what they felt after you had gone. But, Lord, you sent them the Holy Spirit; what about me? You have left me alone. If the Spirit prays in the depth of my being, I know nothing of it. O Lord, send me your Spirit to pray in me and for me, I beseech you!

You showed me your love, Lord, until it was almost an agony. Now you have taken it away. Have mercy on me, Jesus Christ.

God-distance of a choked-up heart

We have first to stand up and face this God-distance of a choked-up heart. We have to resist the desire to run away from it either in pious or in worldly business. We have to endure it without the narcotic of the world, without the narcotic of sins or of obstinate despair. What God is really far away from you in this emptiness of the heart? Not the true and living God; for he is precisely the intangible God, the nameless God; and that is why he can really be the God of your measureless heart. Distant from you is only a God who does not exist: a tangible God, a God of man's small thoughts and his cheap, timid feelings, a God of earthly security, a God whose concern is that the children don't cry and that philanthropy doesn't fall into disillusion, a very venerable idol! That is what has become distant.

Should one not endure such a God-distance as this? Indeed we can truly say: in this experience of the heart, let yourself seemingly accept with calm every despair. Let despair fill your heart so that there no longer seems to remain an exit to life, to fulfilment, to space and to God. In despair, despair not. Let yourself accept everything: in reality it is only an acceptance of the finite and the futile. And no matter how wonderful and great it may have been, let it be really you; your own self, you with your ideals, you with the preliminary estimate of your life (which was sketched out and planned with such shrewd precision), you with your image of God, that satisfied *you* instead of the incomprehensible One himself. Make *yourself* block up every exit; only the exits to the finite, the paths that lead to what is really trackless, will be dammed up. Do not be frightened over the loneliness and abandonment of your interior dungeon, which seems to be so dead—like a grave. For if you stand firm, if you do not run from despair, if in despair over the idols which up to now you called God you do not despair in the true God, if you thus stand firm—this is already a wonder of grace—then you will suddenly perceive that your grave-dungeon only blocks the futile finiteness; you will become aware that your deadly void is only the breadth of God's intimacy, that the silence is filled up by a word without words, by the one who is above all name and is all in all. That silence is God's silence. It tells you that he is there.

Karl Rahner

Grey prayer

Questioner Dear God, prayer is grey, dull, empty, and almost boring. I cannot believe that I am praying at all, though I know I want to pray. What am I to do, Lord?

God You must accept the prayer that I give you. You are praying as a member of my Body and you are sharing in the dullness and emptiness which so many experience today. With me you bear the burdens of others as others help bear yours. Have courage and keep on for I am always with you even in the greyest prayer.

Desolation

Lord. I cannot even visualise you on the cross. All is darkness and I have no sense of your presence, only a numb emptiness. I cannot picture you at all or feel compassion for you. I am in darkness, lost, futile; is this half-deadness, this emptiness, your suffering and mine being mixed together? As I am human, I suppose, my knowledge of God as he is, must be darkness and silence in some way or other. If you, Christ, live in me, perhaps it is not so strange that I have to die with you in loneliness with a sense of futility? Lord, help me to trust that I will also rise with you and know the joy and peace of resurrection.

Lord, when I feel forsaken by you, make me realise that in this desolation I am nearer to you than when I am conscious of your presence. I find it very hard to believe.

Lord, since thou hast taken from all that I had of thee, yet of thy grace leave that gift which every dog has by nature: that of being true to thee in my distress, when I am deprived of any consolation. This I desire more fervently than all thy heavenly kingdom.

Saint Mechthild of Magdebourg (1212-1280)

In the hour of my distress,
When temptations me oppress,
And when I my sins confess,
    Sweet Spirit comfort me!

When the tempter me pursu'th
With the sins of all my youth,
And half damns me with untruth,
    Sweet Spirit comfort me!

When the judgment is revealed
And that opened which was sealed,
When to thee I have appeal'd,
    Sweet Spirit comfort me!

Robert Herrick (1591-1674)

That man is perfect in faith who can come to God in the utter dearth of his feelings and desires, without a glow or an aspiration, with the weight of low thoughts, failures, neglects, and wandering forgetfulness, and say to him: 'thou art my refuge'.

George Macdonald (1824-1905)

This can be a very short prayer indeed. There is only one requirement of a soul when it is in this state—abandonment. I accept this deprivation for your sake. I bow myself entirely to your will. Destitute I wait the return of your favour—even if I have to wait until you reveal yourself to me in the Beatific vision. Now is the time for me to remember what your mother said to Bernadette at Lourdes: 'I have not promised to make you happy in *this* life'. If you give me strength, Lord, I can go on as I am. There is no hurry, the pace is yours.

Hubert van Zeller

When my cross is heavy

Father, when I find the cross very heavy and my way utterly dark, help me to remember how firmly I believe in your love and how I always want to accept your will. When I forget how your love supports me, remind me and strengthen me, for I am very weak and easily lose courage. Make me remember that with the help of your love, your Son, I can do all things.

Dereliction

Lord, you have left me in most horrible darkness and I am in despair. The agony of my dereliction is so great that I have to laugh when I hear your loving kindness spoken of. You seem remote and aloof from my unbearable emptiness. Why have you put me in this misery? The pain and desolation are beyond telling. They tell me that the light of your presence is cleansing my soul and that you wound me through love. I find this impossible to believe. Stop me from going mad and give me strength to survive. But best of all, if you really do care, take me out of this abyss, this well of emptiness!

The Lord: This is the way I treat my friends.
Saint Teresa of Avila: This is why you have so few friends.

Pain of doubting God's existence

Lord, do you exist? I don't know any more. I have gone to church all my life and found it warm and comforting to think of you looking after me and loving me. Now my children tell me I am silly, there is no proof of your existence, and that none of my prayers to you have really been answered. Are they right? I used to think when I prayed you were close to me and helping, now there seems emptiness. Lord, if you are there with me, let me know somehow. I can't go on not knowing, with no certainty; without you my life would seem empty and meaningless. Ease this unbearable pain and somehow give me some sort of faith again.

Unanswered prayer

Your disciples, Lord, told us that you said: 'ask and you shall receive, seek and ye shall find, knock and it shall be opened unto you'. Well, I get an awful ache and disillusion sometimes, because I seem to go on asking and asking and my prayer doesn't get answered. So I twist and turn and ask myself: 'Is it the wrong prayer? Am I asking the wrong way? Am I too sinful to be answered?' Then my thoughts shift and I ask: 'Does God care? Is he faithful to his promise, or even does God exist?' So here I am, depressed, aching, losing heart and trust, and still asking. But this time I'm just going to say to you: 'Lord that I may see; only your will be done'.

Panic in prayer

Dear Lord, this fear is invading my prayer—I can't recollect myself and get peace. Help me, please. Remind me of your presence, asleep in the boat of my soul. I will read again this passage (*Luke 8. 22-23*). Please calm me. 'Rebuke the wind and the turbulent waters' and say 'where is your faith?', remind me that the whole world, and this country, and my friends and my own heart are in your hands. Whatever happens there are people to help and with whom I can share the peace and confidence you give me. In your will is my tranquillity.

B.M.

Jesus, you see that I can't pray any more. Pray for me, Lord, please pray for me.

No man understandeth what love is in itself but, such are its workings, it giveth more than one can take, and asketh more than one can pay.

Jan Ruysbroeck (1293-1381)

He has veiled his love in the stillness of his silence so that our love might reveal itself in faith.

Lord, even if you slay me, yet will I trust you.

Job 13

Oh, night that guided me, Oh, night more lovely than
  the dawn,
Oh, night that joined Beloved with lover, Lover
  transformed in the Beloved.

Saint John of the Cross (1542-1591)

I sought God for thirty years; I thought it was I who desired him, but no, it was he who desired me.

Abu Azid

FOR THE SUFFERING

> O hear my cry, O God;
> attend to my prayer.

Psalm 61.1

Intercession has always been a large part of prayer; indeed so large that it covers a variety of appeal almost as wide as the population of the world from creation till now.

Behind it is the dual idea of God as loving, and man as brother to man. If we accept God as author of life and as provident, then we have a relationship with him which supposes the possibility, even the desirability, of our asking for what we want from him.

Also, our human relationships (one with another) makes it right that we should help each other as best we can. And so we have a way of uniting our efforts in relating to God and asking God for the good of those suffering or in need.

Here particularly there is scope for every individual to express whatever plea is necessary, to do it for another, and to cover the multiplicity of sicknesses, sorrows, pains and wounds. If you are helped to express yourself and feel freer and more able to speak to God what is in your heart, then this section will have achieved its aim.

For the suffering

Lord Jesus, we beseech thee by the loneliness of thy suffering on the cross, be nigh unto all who are desolate and in pain or sorrow today; and let thy presence transform their loneliness into comfort, consolation and holy fellowship with thee, thou pitiful Saviour.

O Lord God, our heavenly Father, regard, we beseech thee, with thy divine pity the pains of all thy children; and grant that the Passion of our Lord and his infinite love may make fruitful for good the tribulations of the innocent, the suffering of the sick, and the sorrows of the bereaved; through him who suffered in our flesh and died for our sake, the same thy Son our Saviour Jesus Christ.

Anonymous

For all in pain

Grant, O Lord, to all those who are bearing pain, thy spirit of healing, thy spirit of peace and hope, of courage and endurance. Cast out from them the spirit of anxiety and fear; grant them perfect confidence in thee, that in thy light they may see light; through Jesus Christ our Lord.

S.P.G.

We bring before thee, O Lord, the griefs and perils of peoples and nations; the necessities of the homeless; the helplessness of the hopeless and weak; the sighings of prisoners; the pains of the sick and the injured; the sorrow of the bereaved. Comfort and relieve them, O merciful Father, according to their needs; for the sake of thy Son our Saviour, Jesus Christ, our Lord.

Attributed to Saint Anselm (1033-1109)

We beseech thee, O Lord, remember all for good; have mercy upon all, O God. Remember every soul who, being in any affliction, trouble, or agony, stands in need of thy mercy and help, all who are in necessity or distress; all who love, or hate us.

Thou, O Lord, art the helper of the helpless; the hope of the hopeless; the saviour of them who are tossed with tempests; the haven of them who sail; be thou all to all. The glorious majesty of the Lord our God be upon us; prosper thou the work of our hands upon us; Oh, prosper thou our handy-work. Lord, be thou within me, to strengthen me; without me, to keep me; above me, to protect me; beneath me, to uphold me; before me, to direct me; behind me, to keep me from straying; round about me, to defend me. Blessed be thou, O Lord, our Father, for ever and ever. Amen.

Lancelot Andrewes (1555-1626)

O thou hope of all the ends of the earth; thou on whom our fathers hoped, and were not confounded; thou, who knowest whereof we are made, and whereby our shortcoming, have pity on us, O Lord. O helper of the helpless, and stronger than the strong, remember all who are in distress of mind, body, or estate; succour them according to their need. It is meet and right, in all things, for all men in joy and sorrow, alone and all together, to remember and worship thee, to trust in thee, and praise thee, Lord and Father, king and God, fountain of life and immortality, source of everlasting good. Thee all the heavens hymn, and higher spirits praise, crying to each other, or going on the work which thou givest them, and so perfecting praise. Blessed be the dweller of eternity, my strength and my deliverer, my salvation and my refuge for ever. Amen.

Rowland Williams (1818-1870)

Let us pray
for those who are deprived and in poverty,
for all who are despairing
and feel themselves to be beyond help,
for all whose minds are disturbed or who are mentally ill,
for those who suffer physically, for years,
and whose bodies are gradually broken down.
Let us pray
for all who must die alone
without the hope of life after death
and without faith in the resurrection of their bodies.

Huub Oosterhuis

We most earnestly beseech thee, O thou lover of mankind, to bless all thy people, the flocks of thy fold. Send down into our hearts the peace of heaven, and grant us also the peace of this life. Give life to the souls of all of us, and let no deadly sin prevail against us, or any of thy people. Deliver all who are in trouble, for thou art our God, who settest the captives free; who givest hope to the hopeless, and help to the helpless; who liftest up the fallen; and who art the haven of the shipwrecked. Give thy pity, pardon, and refreshment to every Christian soul, whether in affliction or error. Preserve us, in our pilgrimage through this life, from hurt and danger, and grant that we may end our lives as Christians, well-pleasing to thee and free from sin, and that we may have our portion and lot with all thy saints. Amen.

Liturgy of Saint Mark

O God, who art the author of love, and the lover of pure peace and affection, let all who are terrified by fears, afflicted by poverty, harassed by tribulation, worn down by illness, be set free by thine indulgent tenderness, raised up by amendment of life, and cherished by thy daily compassion, through Jesus Christ our Lord. Amen.

Gallican Sacramentary

O Lord Jesus Christ, let the light both of thy pains and of thy triumphs shine upon thy servants in suffering and distress, to give them faith in thy good purpose, the support of thy presence, and strong confidence in thy power to heal and save; who art with the Father and the Holy Spirit God everlasting.

Anonymous

For the hungry

O heavenly Father, who by thy blessed Son hast taught us to ask of thee our daily bread: have compassion on the millions of our fellow-men who live in poverty and hunger; relieve their distress; make plain the way of help; and grant thy grace unto us all, that we may bear each other's burden according to thy will; through Jesus Christ our Lord.

George Appleton

O Christ, who being rich, for our sakes wast made poor; King of glory, who didst will to become the man of sorrows: teach us to serve thee in the person of our needy brethren, weak, suffering, and set at naught; in fear lest at the last day we be of those to whom thou shalt say: 'Depart from me'.

Eugène Bersier (1831-1889)

For those in trouble

O God of all mercy and love, I bring before thee all in need of thy help—those in sickness and pain, the dying, the lonely, the sad. Grant that they may all look up to thee, to receive that strength which shall make them more than conquerors, through him that loves us all, even Jesus Christ our Saviour.

George Appleton

For a friend who is mentally distressed

Lord, how can I help my friend who is in such mental distress? I listen to him with as much sympathy as I seem to have. Lord, without you I can do nothing. I have so little; like your apostles I present you my five loaves and two fishes but, Lord, he needs so much more—there are five thousand of him. Help me, work through me with your Spirit, make me understanding, sympathetic beyond my small capabilities and unendingly patient. Fill me with a love that is capable of this, and never let me count the cost beforehand.

O Heavenly Father, who of thy love and wisdom knowest the anxieties and fears of thy children; whose Son Jesus Christ said to his disciples: 'It is I, be not afraid'; and to the tempest: 'Peace be still': grant that this thy servant may be strengthened to cast all his care upon thee, for thou carest for him. Give him quietness; give him unshaken trust; and may the day-spring from on high guide his feet into the way of peace; through the same Jesus Christ our Lord.

Church of Ireland Prayer Book

For the sick in mind

O God, who hast made all men, and lovest all whom thou hast made, we commend into thy gracious care all those who are diseased or deranged in mind. Though their reason be disordered, yet make thyself known to their innermost spirit, and bestow on them thy good gifts of peace and quietness, for the sake of Jesus Christ our Lord and Saviour.

Author unknown

O Holy Spirit, who dost search out all things, even the deep things of God and of man, we pray thee so to penetrate into the springs of personality of all who are sick in mind as to bring them peace and unity and healing. Dispel all anxiety and cast out all fear, that they may be restored to health and glorify thee in lives made whole and free; for the sake of Jesus Christ our Saviour.

George Appleton

O thou who art the Mind of all creation, we remember to our comfort that thou hast in thy special care all broken, outworn and imperfect minds. Give to those who live with them the understanding and loving Spirit of Christ. Enlighten those who are tempted to laugh at such infirmity, or regard it with shame. To all who are separated in this life by barriers of mental infirmity, grant the comfort of thy Holy Spirit, who with thee and thy Christ ever liveth and reigneth, one God, world without end.

Frank Colquhoun

Lord of great compassion, we pray you for those who are nervously ill, and too weak and anxious to lift themselves above the fear and sadness that threaten to overwhelm them. Do you yourself, O Lord, lift them up and deliver them, as you delivered your disciples in the storm at sea, strengthening their faith and banishing their fear. Turning to you, O Lord, may they find you, and finding you may they find also all you have laid up for them within the fortress of your love.

Elizabeth Goudge

For parents of a retarded child

O God of mercy and compassion, behold and bless these people in their need; fold their child in the arms of thy love; take away all bitterness from their hearts and give them patience, kindness, and wisdom to choose wisely for their child who is a whole person in thy sight; in the name of Jesus Christ our Saviour.

Robert N. Rodenmayer

For unwanted children

O God, our Father, we remember before thee all orphaned, homeless and unwanted children, the children of loveless homes, and those who suffer from bodily defect and disease. Make our hearts burn within us for the children of our dark places, and teach us how to turn to good account the laws that protect them and the efforts of those who strive to succour them; through Jesus Christ our Lord.

Mothers' Union

For all men in distress

Lord God,
You are the comfort of the sorrowful and the strength
of the tortured.

Hear the prayers
of all men in distress
and all who appeal to your mercy,
so that they may recognise with joy that you have helped
    them in every ordeal,
through Jesus Christ, our Lord.

Huub Oosterhuis

For the deprived

Lord, I want to pray for the deprived who cannot pray
themselves. It is hard for me who have the love and security
of a family to understand how the deprived feel. I have
creative work which I enjoy while they so often have dull
mechanical jobs. Help me to appreciate how being deprived
can make people angry and violent. Stop me from hating
those who are driven in desperation to violence for reasons
I cannot understand. Use me to help those whose lives lack
love and dignity. If I cannot do this at least give me the kind
of love that is understanding and tolerant.

Intercession for those with crises -

We pray for those facing crises: for young people as they
choose their jobs and decide their way of life; for those who
are embarking on marriage, or have come to some crisis in
marriage; and for parents as they decide things which will
affect their children.

We pray for all whose decisions affect others, whether at
work or in government or in church life. May they survive
the strains of power, be equal to the trust which is placed in
them, and do what they think right without selfishness or
fear.

We pray too for those who in the ordinary course of their
work have seen that something is wrong, and must choose

between drawing attention to it and letting things lie. May they be free from the fear of becoming involved; and yet free too from smugness and malice. May they find satisfaction not in denouncing what is wrong and exposing those responsible, but in stimulating what would be right and encouraging those who could do it.

Father, we are so much the people our actions make us that we ask your help, through the Holy Spirit, in the full round of our personal choices. Especially when things have gone wrong for us, when the pressures of life make us wonder just who we are trying to be, remind us that the future is always with you, who raised Jesus even from the crisis of dereliction and death.

More Contemporary Prayers

For those who have lost faith

Let us pray
for all those who are in great difficulty—
for those who have lost their faith
in man and love, their faith in God,
for those who seek Truth and cannot find it.
Let us pray for married people
who have drifted apart from each other
and for all priests who have broken down
under the strain of their office.

Huub Oosterhuis

Facing an operation

Father of compassion and mercy, who never failest to help and comfort those who cry to thee for succour, give strength and courage to this thy *son* in *his* hour of need. Hold thou *him* up and *he* shall be safe; enable *him* to feel that thou art near, and to know that underneath are the everlasting arms; and grant that, resting on thy protection, *he* may fear no evil, since thou art with him; through Jesus Christ our Lord.

Irish Prayer Book

For the lonely and those shut in on themselves

Lord, help the lonely especially those who find it difficult to communicate with others. Teach me how to help them; how to approach those who are shut up in themselves, are afraid of other people, afraid of being laughed at, of being different. Show me how to draw them out and make them talk and then to listen companionably. Stop me from withdrawing into myself and giving up if I am snapped at when I try to break down barriers.

For the deaf

Lord, we pray for those who cannot hear, and who miss the warm comfort of the human voice, and the beauty of the singing of birds and of music made by man. Though we often complain and are distracted by the noises of the modern world, we would miss them and feel cut off from life if we did not hear them. Lord, help the deaf not to feel isolated and shut in on themselves because they cannot hear. Teach them to come to know you in the stillnesses so that it is not a void of emptiness and isolation for them. Make us patient and understanding of the deaf, and not to think of them as a nuisance just to be avoided. Help us to try to communicate with them in any way which we can and not simply to dodge them.

For the crippled

O Lord Jesus, bound to the pillar and nailed to the cross, we pray thee for those who have lost their physical freedom and can no longer walk with other men and share their work and joy. We pray for those who lie in iron lungs, and all held captive by crippling diseases, all injured in accidents or maimed by war. We remember the young, and we remember too those who have spent many years in pain and weariness. Grant, O Lord, that we who have our freedom may never forget them but may have them always in our hearts and prayers. Knowing ourselves incapable of their courage and cheerfulness, we ask with humility and reverence that the bestowals of your grace may come to them with increasing blessing. Lord, illumine their fortitude and patience with your own, uphold them in your love and possess them with your peace.

Elizabeth Goudge

For the blind

O God, who art the Father of light, with whom is no darkness at all: we thank thee for the good gift of sight which thou hast bestowed upon us. Fill us, we pray thee, with thine own compassion for those who have it not; direct and prosper the efforts that are made for their welfare: reveal to them by thy Spirit the things which eye hath not seen, and comfort them with the hope of light everlasting; to which, of thy great mercy, we beseech thee to bring us all; through Jesus Christ our Saviour.

Arthur W. Robinson

For the dumb

Lord, help the dumb and those who stammer not to feel cut off from others. Help me to be patient with them when they try to communicate and not to dodge them because communicating with them can be so slow and embarrassing as they so often make such odd noises. Lord Jesus, you healed the dumb and deaf and understood their particular misery, make me understanding and considerate to them, and so help to ease their sense of loneliness and isolation.

For old people

Dear God, you made the whole of life to be lived and enjoyed, so please bless all old people. Give them all that they need for friendship, comfort and occupation. Above all give them zest for life and peace in their hearts; through Jesus Christ our Lord.

C. R. Campling

Intercession

We pray for man whose hope is overtaken by disappointment, and whose very striving halts in failure
 —the man who worked so hard to give his family everything and sees his eldest son end up in court;
 —the man who thinks that he will go far, and comes to realise that his best work is done;
 —the man whose life is changed suddenly by accident, curtailed by sickness, or stricken in any way.
We pray for such, who discover that this life is a dying life; that they may discover too the meaning of Easter—that their labour in the Lord cannot be lost.

More Contemporary Prayers

War victims

O God, who hast promised that they that wait upon thee shall renew their strength, we commend to thee all who suffer in this time of war; the wounded, the sick, and the prisoners; the homeless, the hungry, and the oppressed; the anxious, the frightened, and the bereaved. Strengthen them, O Lord, with thy Holy Spirit, and give them friends to help them; we ask it in his name, who bore for us the agony of the cross, thy Son, our Lord Jesus Christ.

Frederick B. Macnutt

For the persecuted

O God, the refuge of the poor, the strength of those who toil, and the Comforter of all who sorrow, we commend to your mercy the unfortunate and needy in whatever land they may be. You alone know the number and extent of their sufferings and trials. Look down, Father of mercies, at those unhappy families suffering from war and slaughter, from hunger and disease, and other severe trials. Spare them, O Lord, for it is truly a time for mercy.

Saint Peter Canisius (1521-1597)

For broken families

Our liberator, you knew the pain of an uncomprehending family. Take up all broken families in your arms; break the chain of misunderstanding and provocation. Teach parents and children gentleness: bring the alienated together by building them into your new community.

The Covenant of Peace

For human casualties

Jesus our brother, you also at the end despaired of the Father: raise up all who have fallen casualties through sickness, anxiety, bitterness, or fear, just as you did in your lifetime on earth; and unite them with us in one movement.

The Covenant of Peace

For the sleepless

Gracious and most merciful Father, let thy presence and peace be known wheresoever there is sickness, sorrow or distress. Give to all tired and weary sufferers this night the gift of sleep; and, if sleep comes not, let thy Holy Spirit bring to their remembrance thoughts of comfort from thy Word, that they may stay their minds on thee, through Jesus Christ our Lord.

The Book of Common Order

For the violent

Lord, I want to pray for those who resort to violence. Help them to see that violence damages people, not only physically but mentally, and that they, themselves, can so easily be hurt in the same way. Make them realise that the victims of violence have friends and relations who love them and that the pain of those hurt may affect whole households. Open the eyes of the violent so that they perceive the wonder of man, and teach them to respect individuals and their feelings. Help and comfort the innocent victims of the passions of men. Lord, make us aware of the forces of evil which so easily can enter into us and possess us, and make us do violence to others.

They enlisted a passer-by, Simon of Cyrene, father of Alexander and Rufus, who was coming in from the country, to carry his cross.

Mark 15.21

An extension of the last section widens the idea that not only can we and should we pray for those who suffer, but we should in such ways as are possible share their suffering or support them in it.

This may seem a whimsical, sentimental idea to some. Perhaps it is best expressed by suggesting that when there is an incurable pain or deep internal grief it can be important to be warmly or silently, yet somehow comfortingly, present with the suffering person.

At such a time various things are necessary. There must be compassion (suffering with) which puts us totally at the service of the other, who may need physically a hug, a long 'sitting with', a shoulder to cry on; or what may be needed is a cup of tea, a gentle soothing to sleep, a patient waiting while nothing happens but perhaps something melts.

We should pray a lot about helping others, asking the Spirit to give us wisdom about how to behave if we are called on for assistance. When this happens we need guidance if we are perplexed about what to say or do next; we need strength of mind, patience and an acceptance of the other person's suffering which will carry us through for however long is necessary.

One of the obstacles to our 'sharing with' is shyness. We may not want to be seen to be sharing or praying with and for one who suffers, or we may be afraid of breaking in on another's loss/pain/suffering. Both attitudes can lead to intense loneliness on the part of the distressed or bereaved person, a sense of being cut off. The single person or family suffering death 'in the house' can almost unwittingly be ostracised.

There is another shyness, which is the shyness of admitting to the suffering or dying person that we really know what is wrong or how bad the situation is. This can lead to false cheerfulness, a false hope of 'how well you look today'. We have to be open to the Spirit and to the sufferer so as to know when to speak and when to be silent. There can be an intense loneliness in 'feeling at death's door' and trying to be cheerful with artificially cheerful people round the bed. The sufferer sometimes knows that they will go away from his bed and 'bury him', while to his face they pretend he is getting better.

Also, it can help a great deal if we pray internally while we are about, and occasionally we may find it possible to draw the sufferer to prayer, to contentment and even to joy.

When considering suffering together and with and for each other we must not forget that we are all members of the body of Christ. Because of this, in some almost inexplicably deep way, we are bound together and do suffer and rejoice together. By prayer and by praying together we can become more aware of this, and the deeper our prayer the more conscious we become of this union. Also we become more aware of the closeness of those who have died in Christ, and how we are interconnected with them and they with us, and how we help each other, and how the saints in heaven and earth support us in our trials and difficulties. We must never forget we are living on this side of the resurrection.

Charles Williams, a close friend of C. S. Lewis, tries in his novel *Descent into Hell* to describe how people can help bear each other's burdens and depicts the inter-connectedness of the living and dead through God in *All Hallows Eve*. For him all the members of the body of Christ, living and dead, are inter-connected with each other and the Persons of the Trinity, or, to use his own term, co-inhere. Time and eternity co-inhere too. Though no section from the novels of

Charles Williams are quoted some readers might find his novels helpful. C. S. Lewis too at the end of his children's book *The Last Battle* gives, in a simpler way, an idea of the inter-relatedness of time and eternity in heaven.

Suffering together

Blessed be the God and Father of our Lord Jesus Christ, the Father of mercies and God of all comfort, who comforts us in all our affliction, so that we may be able to comfort those who are in any affliction, with the comfort with which we ourselves are comforted by God. For as we share abundantly in Christ's sufferings, so through Christ we share in comfort too. If we are afflicted, it is for your comfort and salvation; and if we are comforted, it is for your comfort, which you experience when you patiently endure the same sufferings that we suffer. Our hope for you is unshaken; for we know that as you share in our sufferings, you will also share in our comfort.

2 Corinthians 1. 3-7

We are all bound up together in the bundle of life, for better, for worse, profiting by the good of others, whether predecessors or contemporaries, suffering by their evils, inevitably and involuntarily. All such suffering can broadly be called 'vicarious', since it is borne in the place of others. But it is only the voluntary acceptance of such suffering which makes it 'vicarious' in the fullest sense. Such acceptance, even if it be no more than uncomplaining submission to what cannot be avoided, gives it a new and spiritual quality. But the fullest significance comes from the voluntary choice of suffering, or rather of some end that is seen to involve suffering, for the common good.

H. Wheeler Robinson

Suffering for thyself, in whatsoever way, the suffering hurts thee and is hard to bear. But suffering for God and for God alone, thy suffering hurts thee not nor does it burden thee, for God bears the load.

Meister Eckhart (1260-1328)

Lord, my God! the amazing horrors of darkness were gathered round me, and covered me all over, and I saw no way to go forth; I felt the depth and extent of the misery of my fellow-creatures separated from the Divine harmony, and it was heavier than I could bear, and I was crushed down under it; I lifted up my hand, I stretched out my arm, but there was none to help me; I looked round about, and was amazed. In the depths of misery, O Lord, I remembered that thou art omnipotent; that I had called thee Father; and I felt that I loved thee, and I was made quiet in my will, and I waited for deliverance from thee. Thou hadst pity upon me, when no man could help me; I saw that meekness under suffering was showed to us in the most affecting example of thy Son, and thou taughtest me to follow him, and I said: 'Thy will, O Father, be done!'

John Woolman (1720-1772)

No one lives for himself,
no one dies for himself.
We live and we die
for God, our Lord,
and we are the Lord's.

Huub Oosterhuis

Lord, take me and live in me more fully, so that I may be used by you to help those who suffer. If you are with me, and my selfishness and shyness do not get in the way of your action, perhaps I may be better equipped to help others. Lord, I would like very much to be able to share with the sorrowful and hurt the wonder of your peace which seems to remain with me through all the trials of my life. Lord, give all whom I know to suffer this most wonderful gift of peace and deep joy which passes all human understanding.

For all men of evil will

Peace to all men of evil will. Let there be an end to all vengeance, to all demands for punishment and retribution. Crimes have surpassed all measure. They can no longer be grasped by human understanding. There are too many martyrs. And lay not their sufferings on the scales of justice, Lord, and lay not these sufferings to the torturer's charge, to exact a terrible reckoning from them. Pay them back in a

175

different way. Put down in favour of the executioners, the informers, the traitors and all men of evil will, the courage, the spiritual strength of the others, their humility, their lofty dignity, their constant inner striving and invincible hope, the smile that staunched the tears, their love, their ravaged broken hearts that remained steadfast and confident in the face of death itself, yes, even at the moments of the utmost weakness. Let all this, O Lord, be laid before thee for the forgiveness of sins, as a ransom for the triumph of righteousness. Let the good and not the evil be taken into account. And may we remain in our enemies' memories not as their victims, not as a nightmare, not as haunting spectres, but as helpers in their striving to destroy the fury of their criminal passions. There is nothing more we want of them, and when it is all over, grant us to live among men as men, and may peace come again to our poor earth—peace for men of goodwill and for all others.

A Jewish prisoner in a concentration camp

Dying for others

Constance May not what we call chance, perhaps be the logic of God? Take the death of our dear Mother, for example. Who would have ever thought she would have found it so difficult to die, and that she would make such a bad end! It is almost as though when God gave her a death, he made a mistake about the kind of one he meant for her, just as the woman who looks after a cloakroom at a party or theatre sometimes gives you, not your own things, but somebody else's. Yes, it must have been somebody else's death, a death not made to measure for our Prioress, a death too small for her, so that she couldn't even get her arms into the sleeves . . .

Blanche Somebody else's death? What does that mean?

176

Constance It means that when death comes to someone, she will be surprised to find how easy it is to die, and will feel at ease and comfortable. She may even boast about it and say: 'See how easily death sits on me; what beautiful folds it makes'.

George Bernanos ('*The Carmelites*')

Intercession at the foot of the Cross

Lord, teach me how to suffer with others as your mother and Saint John suffered with you at the foot of the cross. Suffering in this way can be deeply painful and I will often want to run away and avoid the troubled and ill, so support me, Lord. Help me to be quietly sympathetic and loving so that I am a comfort to sufferers. Speak through me so I may say what is needed to help. If I am drained and exhausted by this waiting by the cross, turn my eyes towards you so that I may not think of myself and complain, but may be filled with love for you who suffered so much for us.

For a restless person

Lord, he is never still, always fidgeting, never at peace. This can so easily irritate and I can get restless and disturbed too. Lord, let him catch the peace you give me even if it means my having to take on myself his restlessness. Lord, be with me in this difficult kind of sharing.

For a sick friend

Lord, my friend is ill and in pain. There is nothing that I can do for him except sit beside him and commend him to your keeping. This is the best thing to do for I know he is safe in your hands, and knowing this brings me peace and comfort. Let him too experience something of this love and peace with which you surround us, and which can even come to underlie pain and make it more bearable.

Lord, teach me how to be comforting to those who are in pain or in great sorrow. Help me so to understand their distress as to be able to share in it in some way. Show me how to have this special kind of openness even though it is costing and wearying for me. And when I am lonely or sad, let others help me in this way too, so that we may truly bear each others' burdens.

Lord, make me sympathetic and compassionate as I listen to her endless grumbles. Let me understand her troubles, help me to love her and give her my whole attention even if this is draining and emptying. Lord, let her know I want to share even her imagined difficulties, and that she is not alone.

Suffering together

Lord, you suffered for us on the cross. We who are your body on earth, in some way share in your sufferings for the world, for ourselves, for our neighbours. Show us how we are to share in these sufferings. For some it will be help of a practical kind; others will have to suffer compassionately alongside people in a helpless kind of way, by being understanding and loving; others perhaps will share their pain deeply in prayer. In whatever way you lead us, deepen our understanding of you and ourselves so that we will be of increasing help in sharing the burdens of the world.

Suffering for others

Lord, you have shown me how I am helped and supported by others who are in union with you, but you did not make it clear to me that I would have to suffer with, and sometimes, even for, others. Lord, it is very hard—I am drained and emptied by the pains of others. Bearing each others' burdens is all very well when it is my burden which is being carried, but this suffering which I am bearing now eats into the depth of my being and drains me of energy. And no one comes to help me and to share the bearing with me. Lord, I cry to you from the depths; help me and strengthen me that I may be able to strengthen others.

Lord, make us realise that by simply suffering for Jesus' sake and by bearing 'about in our bodies the dying of Jesus' we can often do more for him and for others than we can by being active. It is very hard to understand this, so please make us realise that our very helplessness can be of great help to others if we suffer it with and for Jesus.

Our suffering works mysteriously, first in ourselves by a kind of renewal and also in others who are perhaps far away, without our ever knowing what we are accomplishing . . . Christ on the cross has perhaps done more for humanity than Christ speaking and acting in Galilee or Jerusalem. Suffering creates life. It transforms everything it touches.

Elizabeth Leseur (1866-1914)

Trying to help a sick friend

Lord, she is asleep; help her, let her know that you love her and that she is in your care. I keep her in my prayer, Lord, and want to share her pain in whatever way you think best. Teach me how to do this, for without your Spirit it is not possible to be deeply compassionate.

179

Watching others suffer

Jesus, I have to watch people suffering, and there seems so little that I can do to help. Lord, show me what to do and what to say. Take my very helplessness and in some way use it to help the suffering. Your mother and your beloved disciple who watched by you when you were dying knew the pain of being utterly useless when someone they loved was dying. Lord, give me the kind of strengthening compassion which they had and which can make suffering less lonely and more bearable. And, Lord, ease the pain of those whom I watch with by giving them a sense of your strengthening presence.

For those battered by life

Lord, help us to heal the wounds of those who are battered by the hardships of life, those who come from broken homes, those whom other people have ill-treated, those who feel themselves to be inferior, those who cannot relate to others. Use us to give them a sense of security. Make us strong so that we can give of our strength to give them confidence, and to bind up and heal their wounded souls and minds. Amen.

All human souls are deeply interconnected . . . we cannot only pray but suffer for each other . . . Nothing is more real than this interconnection, this gracious power put by God himself into the very heart of our infirmities.

Baron von Hügel (1832-1925)

I believe that there circulates among souls—those here below, those expiating their sins, and those who have attained true life—a vast and ceaseless stream of the sufferings, merits, and love of all these souls; and that even our slightest pains, our least sorrows, can, through the Divine action, reach out to souls both dear and distant and bring them light and peace and holiness.

Elizabeth Leseur (1866-1914)

Communion of Saints

Lord, help us to perceive that we are all linked together through you, and that because of our union with you, we share each others' burdens and joys. Lord, make us realise that we are never alone in suffering for you and all our brothers are with us in it. By our prayers for each other made through you and by the prayers of the saints on earth and in heaven, make us conscious of the great support we have as members of your Body. Lord, I thank you for the most wonderful gift of the communion of Saints.

Lord, I thank you for letting me see, if dimly, the unity of all Christian people which transcends ordinary sight. I perceive how we are all bound together in some inexplicable way, and how all our prayers are interconnected, how we can suffer with each other, bear each other's burdens, and rejoice together. I thank you for letting me see that we truly form one body. You strengthen me by letting me know that I am never alone because you and the company of the faithful departed are always supporting me though I cannot always perceive this. Help me to impart to others this wonderful sense of the one-ness of all Christians, both alive and dead, for it is not easy to explain in human terms.

Jesu, Eternal Priest, take our lives into your divine hands, as little accidents consecrated to your glory; bless, and if need be, break and speak over them words of unspeakable wonder and condescension, by which it may no longer be we who live, but our Lord who lives and reigns in us. And if our lives have already been broken or wasted, help us, blessed martyrs and apostles, by your example and prayers, to fulfill Christ's bidding, and gather up the fragments that remain. Perhaps by a miracle of omnipotent love and pity, he will multiply our efforts, so that we will be able to bring more than in the beginning to serve his high mysterious purposes.

William Howard (17th century)

Lord Jesus, you have told us that we are to be perfect as our Father in heaven is perfect. We know that we cannot do this without your grace and the power of the Spirit. And when we look at our world, there are so many discouragements to our perfection. But we thank you for all the saints of every age and of every nation who show us the way, through joy, through sorrow, through seeming defeat and seeming success, to become like you and thus to shine as lights of the world. With them, whether in this world or beyond it, we thank and praise you. We are one body with many members, through whom your Spirit works to lead all mankind to you.

E.S.A.

THE LIFE

PRAYERS OF THOSE SERIOUSLY ILL OR DYING

Jesus, Son of David, have mercy on me.

Mark 10. 25

It always seems to us to be a sad reflection on the state of our human development that we hide death, especially that we hide it from those who are dying.

There will certainly be those that take the opposing view, but surely they cannot be numbered among believers in heaven, resurrection and Jesus Christ?

We are reminded of the words of a priest who was quite consciously and peacefully living through the last weeks of incurable cancer. He spoke of the goodness of the people of his parish, how they visited him, and how they told him that they prayed he would get better. But, he said, he always replied that this was like telling someone you were praying that his summer holidays would be cancelled!

There are of course many angles to serious illness and the possible approach of death. But it is at least arguable that a person will be more of a person if he or she faces the prospect of death rather than pretending that it will not happen. This need not, should not, be a morbid dwelling on death, but realism flowing from and into hope in Christ the healer, and hope in Christ the resurrection.

The apostle James says: 'Is anyone sick among you? Let him call in the priests of the church . . .' If we are pretending you are not ill we can hardly expect this added help from the church. But if you seriously face the issue of health, and life and death in faith, prayer can be a tremendous strength, peace and joy-bearer.

We would therefore like to offer this section especially to those who are in sickness, who may be lost, who cannot feel how to pray, or who are secretly afraid.

Jesus spent a lot of time with the sick in his life in this world. To understand his care is to lose any sense of shame and humiliation at growing incapacity, incontinence and so on.

If those living with the sick or visiting them in hospital were encouraged by the sick person to pray with them at the bedside, a barrier would be broken down and a new dimension enter into their lives.

The section should be taken in conjunction with most of the other sections, for they will all fit in, once the shyness to begin is overcome.

For patience in suffering

It was dark, Mary, when you fled to Egypt with your Son in order to escape Herod's soldiers. It was dark when he was twelve and you thought you'd lost him as you returned from the Passover feast. It was dark when he seemed to rebuke you—'Woman what have I to do with thee?' It was darkest when you stood at the foot of his cross and saw him die a criminal's death. That must have seemed an eternity of darkness. Yet at the blackest of all moments you were closest to the light—only three days from Easter: the blinding, dazzling light of power and strength and joy.

Sometimes *I* seem to be escaping with Jesus in my arms, able to share my pain with his or to feel his sharing mine. At other times in my pain and loneliness I am bewildered and seem to have lost him. Sometimes everything seems so black and hopeless that I think he has turned me away. I get glimpses of Easter because my pain is on the other side of it in time to yours, but I still have my periods of darkness.

Please pray for me, Mary, that I may persevere, even to the foot of the cross. Pray that I may show your Son a little of the love you gave him. I know in my innermost heart light will shine. And what are three days, three years or three decades of waiting in God, eternity?

J.A.I.O.

As I lie here, pretty well unable to think or pray, I love to hold a crucifix, Lord. In some way this contact soothes me and keeps me one with your suffering, Jesus Christ.

Lord, I'm weak, I'm tired. O help me, Lord.

They say the operation will be a major one, Lord. I had to be persuaded to have it, but now I have been anointed and a great peace has come in. I want to relax and rest in you, but the old me kicks and squirms and fights. Please let your peace keep me.

I know I've got cancer, Lord. It is eating its way through me, catching me here and there. I think I've got it on the run, but even so, I want to say, your will not mine.

I wish I suffered better, Lord. I wish I was always cheerful, patient, smiling. But I know I groan at pain. Always I seem to be wanting something and to be dissatisfied when I get it. I snap at the nurses and doctors, especially when they say I seem so much better and I know I am so much worse. Guide me, lead me, love me, Lord.

I hold the crucifix in my hand, Lord. I can't manage much else, and I can't think or pray any more. But just to hold it Lord, and to remember you've been through pain and death before me. It helps: help me—but only according to your will, if I have the courage to go on saying that.

I haven't the energy to pray, Lord. God knows what my temperature is. It feels like the end. I'm so tired. Must I go on breathing, wouldn't you bring it all to an end? O Lord, I'm so tired, nothing comes, too tired even to fear. So tired, Lord, so tired. . .

Sickness and fear of death

Lady, help! Jesu, mercy!
    The fear of death perturbs me.

Dread of death, sorrow of sin
    Troubles my heart full grievously;
My soul disturbed by sinful desires, then
    Passion of Christ strengthen me.

For blindness is a heavy thing,
    And to be deaf therewith especially,
To lose my light and my hearing—
    Passion of Christ strengthen me;

And to lose my taste and my smelling,
    And to be sick in my body;
Here I have lost all my liking—
    Passion of Christ strengthen me.

Thus God he gives and takes away,
    And, as he will, so must it be.
His name be blest both night and day—
    Passion of Christ strengthen me.

Here is a cause of great mourning;
    Of myself I nothing see
Save filth, uncleanness, vile stinking—
    Passion of Christ strengthen me.

Into this world no more I brought;
    No more I have with me truly
Save good deed, word, will and thought—
    Passion of Christ strengthen me.

The five wounds of Jesu Christ
    My medicine now must they be,
The fiends' power down to cast—
    Passion of Christ strengthen me.

As I lay sick in my languor,
    With sorrow of heart and tear of eye,
This carol I made with great dolour—
    Passion of Christ strengthen me.

Oft' with this prayer I me blest:
    In your hands, Lord,
Thou take my soul into thy rest—
    Passion of Christ strengthen me.

Learn this lesson of blind Audelay:
    When trouble is highest, the cure may come.
If you be troubled night or day,
    Say: 'Passion of Christ comfort me'.

John Audelay (15th century)

Two weeks ago I had a coronary, Lord. It is on the mend, but I know it is likely I'll never be quite the same again, and I suppose I could die quite suddenly. At first I resented this and was frightened and angry with you. Now I'm a bit calmer but at night especially I get great gusts of fear and see lifetimes of sleeplessness. I don't really know what to ask for; courage, serenity, peace, recovery, a happy death? Perhaps all of these and more. You know, Lord, what I need. Hear my prayer.

Fear of dying

Lord, I love you very much and really do want to be with you always, but I am afraid of dying. Give me the kind of faith in you that will not waver, the kind of hope which will help me to believe that you will be with me even to the end of the world, and the kind of love that will trust you completely whatever happens. Keep me in peace and guard me from fear, for the sake of your dear Son who knows human frailty so well.

Lord, help me.

Into your hands, O Lord, I commend my spirit.

Lord Jesus, receive my soul.

I do not know if I will live or die; not one will tell me. They smile and say how much better I look today and, Lord, I feel ghastly. Give me peace, Lord. Your will be done.

So sudden, Lord. Yesterday I was well, then they say I had a stroke; now I move little but can concentrate a bit. Lord, I ask that I may get well or die, not just hang about, as a nuisance to everyone. It's up to you, Lord.

O God,
I think that everyone has done all that can be done,
     and I have the feeling
     that it is not enough.
So I'm coming to you now
     because I have nowhere else to go.
Make me quite sure that, whatever happens,
nothing can separate me from you,
that, whether I get better or not,
I am in your hands.
Help me,
     not to be afraid any more,
     and not to worry any more.
I'm not giving in:
I'll still hold on to life
     and do everything to get well.
But make me sure that,
     whether I live or die,
you are with me always,
     to the end—and beyond the end.
Let me remember the faith of the Psalmist:
     In peace I will both lie down and sleep,
     for thou alone, O Lord, makest me dwell in safety.

William Barclay

Have mercy on me in my last end

   O blessed Jesu, most mighty lion, king immortal and
victorious, have mind of the sorrow that thou sufferedst
when all the powers of thine heart and body for feebleness
failed thee utterly. And when thou saidst, inclining thine
head thus: 'It is all done'. For mind of thine anguish and
sorrow blessed Jesu, have mercy on me in my last end, when
my soul shall be anguished and my spirit troubled. So be it.

Saint Bridget of Sweden

Lord, I am dying now. There is so much I wanted to do, so much I never did. I look back on life and think if only . . . But now, Lord, I'm tired. I can't think properly. Let me give everything over to you, sort it out for me, dear Lord, that I may rest in peace.

I never thought I should be so afraid, Lord. I said I loved you and I wanted to be with you, but now it's happening I'm all confused and frightened. I know you so well, Lord, and yet I hardly know you. It's a bit like marrying again, a leap in faith, a union for ever. Give me courage, give me peace.

Lord, I'm dying by inches. I know it may take months or even years: on the other hand, something could give way suddenly, and I might die in my sleep. But the doctors have made me aware of the possibilities and I'm grateful for that. So I want first to thank you for the gift of that knowledge. It is so much better, more fully human, than doubt. Next I want to thank you for the gift of the life I have had and am having. It has been wonderful, O God, wonderful! Of course, there have been hellish times too, but there is so much to thank you for in creation, in people, in relationships of love. And now, I just want to ask you that however long you give me here, and however much I loathe my illness, I may use it fully and lovingly for you and all those who surround me—family, friends and everyone else. Give me faith, hope and love.

I know I'm going to die. I know it comes to everybody. Part of me knows that you are there, Lord, and says: 'I love you'. But there is still this cold, quaking feeling, this unknown fear of the unknown; there is the parting and the 'losing' of friends. Oh, I know it's silly and it means somehow I do not love you as fully as I should. And yet, and yet, it is difficult, Lord. So can you let me look at it calmly and give your Spirit to me that I may understand more, and be able to go forward peacefully and even joyfully into the shadow of death through which there gleams new life? Amen.

Lord, I am afraid of dying. I think I love you and want to be with you but the thought of going from this world into the unknown is terrifying. I begin to wonder if you exist. O Lord, help me, give me some reassurance that you will be with me unto the end of the world and beyond it into the next.

Lord in the depth of the night a terrible panic hits me. I feel I'm dying. Sometimes I can't breathe, or I think my heart is stopping. It is so terrible, I get up and walk about and go into the street to be with some living being. But now I'm afraid to go out because of all this 'mugging'. So I am shut in and dead scared. Lord, reassure me, give me calm, take away fear.

Lord, now that I am coming to the final parting on this earth, I am afraid that I will lose for ever those whom I love deeply. Lord, let me be united with them even more closely in the next life. Help them to go on remembering me with love when I die; never let us lose each other. So many people left on earth seem to forget their friends who die; do not let this happen with me. Give me faith to realise that this is not a final parting and that we will all be united in your kingdom where love reigns completely.

Am I dying?

Lord, I've always tried to avoid looking too closely at the future in case it might be unpleasant, now I am not sure whether I want to know if I am going to die or not. Yet I'd rather know, but can't bring myself to ask the doctor. Please give me strength to do this, because I'd really like to know how soon I am going to come to you; for I do want to, even if I am a little fearful of dying.

Preparation for death

O Creator and sovereign of all beings, but especially of man, thy peculiar workmanship; O God of thine own people their parent and their ruler; O arbiter of life and death; O guardian and benefactor of our souls: thou that createst and changest all things, by thine energising word, as it seemeth best in the depths of thy wisdom and administration . . . mayst thou receive us hereafter, in thine appointed hour, having ruled us in the flesh, as long as it subserved our spiritual welfare; and oh! may we arise prepared to meet our judge; not perturbed, nor recoiling with affright from the closing day of nature, like those who are lovers of the world and lovers of the body; but joyfully ascending to the blessed and sempiternal life; that life which is in Jesus Christ, unto whom is due the homage of exhaustless ages.

Saint Gregory Nazienzen (325-090)

Repentance before death

The praise of God at the beginning and in the end, he does not reject. He does not refuse him who attempts it—the only Son of Mary, the Lord of princes. He will come like the sun, from the east to the north. Mary Mother of

192

Christ, glory of maidens, intercede in thy great mercy with thy Son to cast out our sins. God be above us, God before us, God who rules, the Lord of Heaven, may he give us a share of mercy. O Lordly hearted One, may there be peace between us without rejection, and may I make amends for all the sins I have committed. Before going to my tomb, to my green grave, in the darkness without candle, to my grave-mound, to my recess, to my hiding place, to my repose, after horses and trolling the pale mead, and carousel, and consort with women, I shall not sleep, I will take thought for my end. We are in a world of grievous wantonness; like leaves from the treetops it will pass away. Woe to the miser who amasses great wealth, and unless he devotes it to God though he be suffered in the course of this world, there will be peril at his end. The fool knows not in his heart how to tremble, he does not rise early, he does not pray, he does not keep vigil, he does not chant prayers, he does not crave mercy; pride and arrogance and pomp, bitterly will they be paid for in the end. He plumps his body but for toads and snakes and lions, and practises iniquity; but Death will come in through the door and ravenously it will gather him up and carry him off. Old age and infirmity of mind draw nigh, your hearing, your sight, your teeth are failing, the skin of your fingers becomes wrinkled, old age and grey hairs do this to you. May Michael intercede for us with the Lord of Heaven for a share of mercy . . .

On hill, in dale, in the islands of the sea, in every way one goes, there is no seclusion from the blessed Christ. My Friend, my Intercessor, it was my desire to attain to the land far away where thou wentest. Seven and seven score and seven hundred saints have gone to the one Tribunal, and in the presence of the blessed Christ they have endured no terror. The gift I ask, may it not be denied me, peace between me and God; may I find the road to the Gate of Glory, Christ, may I not be sad before thy Throne.

Anonymous Welsh author (12th century)

Heavenly and eternal Father, source of all being, from whom I spring, unto whom I shall return, thine I shall ever be. Thou wilt call me unto thyself when my hour comes. Blessed shall I then be if I can say: 'I have fought a good fight'. I fear not death, O Father of life; for death is not eternal sleep; it is the transition to a new life, a moment of glorious transformation, an ascension towards thee. How could that be an evil that cometh from thy hand, when thou art the all-good! Lord of life and death, I am in thy hand; do unto me as thou deemest fit; for what thou dost is well done. When thou didst call me from nothing into life, thou didst will my happiness; when thou callest me away from life, will my happiness be less thy care? No, no, thou art love, and whosoever dwells in love, dwells in thee, O Lord, and thou in him. Amen.

Heinrich Tschokke (1771-1848)

As death approaches

Lord, you have loved me and have supported me all the days of my life, and I trust you. Now that the time of my death approaches, give me faith to trust you still and to know that you will continue to support me as you have always done. Death like life comes from you and like all your gifts must be good, so take away any fears I may have. When death comes to hush my last breath on earth, help me to remember that it will bring me to live more fully with you and this is the most wonderful thing that can happen to me, so into your hands I commend my spirit.

For death to come soon

O my Saviour and my God, let it come: let it come, I pray thee, the hour when I may at length gladden mine eyes with

194

the vision of what I now believe; may apprehend what now I hope for and greet from afar; may with my spirit embrace and kiss what now with my whole might I yearn after, and be altogether absorbed in the abyss of thy love. And meanwhile bless, O my soul, my Saviour, and magnify his name, which is holy and full of the holiest delights.

Saint Anselm (1033-1109)

The Lord has given, the Lord has taken away. Blessed be the name of the Lord.

Father, into thy hands I commend my spirit.

Prayers at the time of dying

Lord, thou dost summon me to thyself, and I am coming to thee, not by my own merits, but solely through thy mercy, which mercy I crave from thee in virtue of thy blood. Father, into thy hands I commend my soul and my spirit.

Saint Catherine of Siena (1347-1389)

O wonderful, O incomprehensible abyss of the love of God.

Benet of Canfield (1562-1611)

Lord, forsake me not, now my strength faileth me. Lord, grant me mercy, for the merits of my Jesus. Now, Lord, receive my soul.

George Herbert (1593-1633)

The last prayer

Before the beginning thou hast foreknown the end,
    Before the birthday the death-bed was seen of thee:
Cleanse what I cannot cleanse, mend what I cannot mend,
    O Lord All-Merciful, be merciful to me.

While the end is drawing near I know not mine end.
    Birth I recall not, my death I cannot foresee:
O God, arise to defend, arise to befriend,
    O Lord All-Merciful, be merciful to me.

Christina Rossetti (1830-1894)

I acknowledge unto thee, O Lord, that both my cure and
my death are in thy hands. If my death be determined by
thee, I will in love accept it at thy hand. Make known to me
the path of life: in thy presence is fullness of joy. Into thy
hands I commend my spirit. Amen and Amen.

Hebrew Prayer Book (abbreviated)

Lo, Lord I come.

Thou, Lord, art with me, and I will not fear.

Hebrew Prayer Book

A dying man's words to the doctors and his wife

I want to go, I want to be with God! Let me go! I'm
sorry, love, I love you very much but I want to go to God.

Dying words of a fifteen-year-old boy

Will you ask God to take away a little of the pain? . . .
I'm dying now. Why are you crying? There is nothing to cry
about! Jesus! Jesus! I'm not swearing, I'm praying.

Dying

Who will rid me of the burden of the flesh?

Saint Paul

Lord, it is not easy for a man to die. We cling to life and
have so little trust in you. Lord, I have been with a man who
did not want to die; he struggled to live. It was painful to
watch. I do not think he believed in you. Teach me what to
pray when this happens again. Show me how to pray in a
way that will bring peace and hope to the dying. Can you,
who were able to strengthen and give hope to the dying
thief, not use me in this sort of way? At least give me a
strong living faith that will support those who are afraid at
the time of death. And when my turn comes give me peace
and complete trust in you.

For me to live is Christ, to die is a gain.

I long to be dissolved and to be with Christ.

Come, Lord Jesus.

DEATH, THE LAST HUMAN PARTING

Now, Master, you can let your servant go in peace, just as you promised.

Luke 2.29

Death is round us, with us, in us. That could be a very gloomy thought, but if we accept its reality, this can change. Instead of pretending, as many people do (which is a non-sense and unworthy of a reasoning human being) that there is no death, we should accept and live with the idea of it, in hope.

What does this mean in simple terms? It rather depends upon belief. If you believe that death is the end after which there is only oblivion, a sleep without dreams or waking, then you will only welcome death as you might welcome sleep; tired you seek rest, anxious you seek escape in a blackout of the senses, suicidal you put an end to depression and care. But, if you believe in God, then death is indeed a dark tunnel or a gateway, but it leads to a new land and a new life.

Death seems so final. For those who get a chance to reflect on their own death, because they are suffering an illness which they know to mean the end of life on earth, there is a special hope of freedom, a new well-being and fulfilment in believing.

In such an individual a new and deeper spiritual dimension can grow and develop, if they, in their circumstances, respond to God. This leads, not to a resentment at dying, nor a resignation to dying, but to a time of deep and growing longing to be with Christ in resurrection.

There is here no denial of the goodness of living or of the beauty of the world; but rather there is an interest and a love of life that is almost infectious. There is no pretending that there is no pain or distress and even fear; but there is a living positiveness running through it all, with the sureness of continuing love and care both now and after death from God and other people.

Death, in the past, has so frequently been covered up in black, full of personal grief and mourning attitudes, which partly stressed the sinful in man and partly the human this-world sorrow at physical parting and dissolution. Today, in less believing circles, there is a tendency to cover up and hide death, for it to be almost a stigma on a family to have a death in the house . . . it is not quite nice.

But any true believer must try to face up to death so as to grow in a sense of the resurrection, and this is the approach that the Church is stressing again today.

Therefore, as we face the parting of death in our prayer, in our thinking or in life itself, let us be more and more in the company of Jesus Christ, who at the tomb of a friend said: 'I am the resurrection'.

One final thing, if death comes next door, or down the road, do not keep away and ostracise the family. It may be a very difficult time to try to get anything across, or even to make some contact, but this is a time when there is a real need of neighbours who care and who will be about, be friendly, and not try to preach resignation, but just to be there as and when needed.

Heavenly Father

Man dies, and this world dies; but nothing can bring your love to an end. Your love would grasp and hold us so that we too should outlive this world's tragedy.

Forgive us, that we have been frightened by death and parting, as if it were the final fact. Forgive us, that the nerve of our faith has broken; and that, seeing no definite answers, we have thought there was no answer, and have been overwhelmed by the futility of the things of this world.

Forgive us, and let us see that you have touched your
kingdom with immortality, and called us into it. Through
Jesus Christ, our Lord.

More Contemporary Prayers

And thou, most kind and gentle death,
Waiting to hush our latest breath.
O praise him, alleluia!
Thou leadest home the child of God
And Christ our Lord the way hath trod.
O praise him, O praise him,
Alleluia, alleluia, alleluia!

Saint Francis of Assisi (1182-1226)

So death will come to fetch you? No not death, but God
himself. Death is not the horrible spectre we see represented
in pictures. The catechism teaches us that death is the
separation of the soul from the body; that is all. I am not
afraid of a separation that will unite me for ever with God.

Saint Theresa

If the grain of wheat does not die . . .
Few words are as consoling as these
Because they incorporate us into the cycle of the universe
Justifying even idle dreams.
All beauty, all life is born
Out of sorrow and decay.

All labour pains are necessary
That the marvel of a human child
Can come into being.

Even amid rotting débris
The most exquisite flower can grow.
Every plant is born of decay.

Death alone will give to us
The life that will establish us
In that world which is our true home country.

Henry Rohr

Eternal and most glorious God, suffer me not so to under-value myself as to give away my soul, thy soul, thy dear and precious soul, for nothing; and all the world is nothing, if the soul must be given for it. Preserve therefore, my soul, O Lord, because it belongs to thee, and preserve my body because it belongs to my soul. Thou alone dost steer my boat through all its voyage, but hast a more especial care of it, when it comes to a narrow current, or to a dangerous fall of waters. Thou hast a care of the preservation of my body in all the ways of my life; but, in the straits of death, open thine eyes wider, and enlarge thy Providence towards me so far that no illness or agony may shake and benumb the soul. Do thou so make my bed in all my sickness that, being used to thy hand, I may be content with any bed of thy making. Amen.

John Donne (1573-1631)

Lord God,
you have made us mortal and we must die.
Do not, we beseech you,
take our lives away for ever,
you who are a God of the living.
We ask you this for Jesus' sake,
today and every day,
for ever and ever.

Huub Oosterhuis

Death, be not proud, though some have called thee
Mighty and dreadful, for thou art not so;
For those, whom thou think'st thou dost overthrow,
Die not, poor Death . . .
One short sleep past, we wake eternally.
And Death shall be no more: Death thou shalt die.

John Donne (1573-1631)

So be my passing!
My task accomplished and the long day done,
My wages taken, and in my heart
Some late lark singing,
Let me be gathered to the quiet west,
The sundown splendid and serene,
Death.

William Henley (1849-1903)

Hear me, O Lord, and remember now that hour in which
thou didst once commend thy blessed spirit into the hands of
thy heavenly Father: when with a torn body and a broken
heart, thou didst show forth the bounty of thy mercy, and
die for us. I beseech thee, O thou Brightness and Image of
God, so to assist me by this thy most precious death, that
being dead unto the world, I may live only to thee; and at
the last hour of thy departing from this mortal life, I commend my soul into thy hands, and thou mayest receive me
into life immortal, there to reign with thee for ever and ever.
Amen.

John Cosin (1594-1672)

O Lord, Jesus Christ, Son of the living God, who at the
evening hour didst rest in the sepulchre, and didst thereby
sanctify the grave to be a bed of hope to thy people, make
us so to abound in sorrow for our sins, which were the cause
of thy passion, that when our bodies lie in the dust, our

souls may live with thee; who livest and reignest with the Father and the Holy Ghost, one God, world without end.

Compline

Jesu, may thy cross defend me,
And thy saving death befriend me,
    Cherished by thy deathless grace:
When to dust my dust returneth,
Grant a soul that to thee yearneth
    In thy Paradise a place.

Stabat mater dolorosa;
ascribed to Jacopone da Todi (d. 1306)

Though I am dead grieve not for me with tears,
Think not of death with sorrowing and tears;
I am so near that every tear you shed touches and
    tortures me though you think me dead.
But when you laugh and sing in glad delight, my soul
    is lifted upward to the light.
Laugh and be glad for all that life is giving and I,
though dead, will share your joy in living.

Anonymous

For rest and peace

O Lord, who art the shadow of a great rock in a weary land, who beholdest thy weak creatures, weary of labour, weary of pleasures, weary of heart from hope deferred, and weary of self. In thine abundant compassion and unutterable tenderness bring us we pray thee, unto thy rest, through Jesus Christ, thy Son, our Saviour.

Christina Rossetti (1830-1895)

For the dying

O Saviour Divine, into thy loving and merciful hands we commend the souls of the dying. By thy most precious death which was our life, forsake not thy servants who have now none other helper beside thee. Receive their spirits, and bring them into thy presence, that the darkness may light about them, and that they may behold thy face in righteousness and be satisfied when they wake with thy likeness. Hear our cry we humbly beseech thee, O Lord Christ.

Anonymous (20th century)

O Lord Jesus Christ, who in thy last agony didst commend thy spirit into the hands of thy heavenly Father, have mercy upon all sick and dying persons; may death be unto them the gate of ever-lasting life; and give them the assurance of thy presence even in the dark valley; for thy name's sake who art the resurrection and the life, and to whom be glory for ever.

Adapted from the Sarum Primer

For the dying

Unto thee, O Lord, we commend the soul of thy servant *N* that, dying unto this world he may live unto thee: and that whatsoever sins he hath committed through human frailty, by thy merciful passion may be wiped away. May his portion this day be in peace and his dwelling in the heavenly Jerusalem; through Christ our Lord.

Guild of Saint Raphael

Prayer at the departing of a soul

Depart, O Christian soul, out of this world,
In the name of God the Father almighty who created thee,
In the name of Jesus Christ who redeemed thee,
In the name of the Holy Ghost who sanctifieth thee.
May thy rest be this day in peace, and thy dwelling
   in the Paradise of God.

                         William Bright (1824-1901)

O Lord and Master and Governor of all, Father of our Lord Jesus Christ, who desirest not the death of a sinner, but rather that he may turn from his wickedness and live, willing that all men should be saved and come to the knowledge of the truth, we pray thee to loose the soul of thy servant *N* from every bond, and to free him from every unfulfilled pledge which he has given, granting him forgiveness of all his sins from his youth till now, known and unknown, in deed and in word, both those which he has sincerely confessed, and those which he has concealed through forgetfulness or shame.

For thou alone loosest bonds and restorest the downtrodden, thou art the hope of them that are in despair, mighty in forgiving the sins of every creature who puts his trust in thee. O Lord, the Lover of mankind, bid him to be released from all the bonds of sin and the flesh. Receive in peace the soul of this thy servant *N* and give him rest in thine eternal dwelling with thy saints, by the grace of thine only son our Lord and God and Saviour, Jesus Christ, with whom thou art blessed together with thine all-holy, gracious and life-giving Spirit now and for ever and unto ages of ages. Amen.

                             Russian Orthodox

When a person has just died

Into thy hands, O merciful Saviour, we commend the soul of thy servant, now departed from the body. Acknowledge, we humbly beseech thee, a sheep of thine own fold, a lamb of thine own flock, a sinner of thine own redeeming. Receive him into the arms of thy mercy, into the blessed rest of everlasting peace, and into the glorious company of the saints in light.

John Cosin (1596-1672)

Give rest, O Christ, to thy servant with thy saints: where sorrow and pain are no more; neither sighing, but life everlasting.

Thou only art immortal, the Creator and Maker of man; and we are mortal, formed of the earth, and unto the earth shall we return: for so didst thou ordain when thou createst me, saying: 'Dust thou art, and unto dust shalt thou return'. All we go down to the dust; and weeping o'er the grave, we make our song: alleluya, alleluya, alleluya.

Give rest, O Christ to thy servant with thy saints, where sorrow and pain are no more; neither sighing, but life everlasting.

Russian Kontakion of the Departed

For the departed

Quicken, O Lord, our departed in thy compassion, and set them at thy right hand. Clothe them with excellent glory in thy kingdom, and join them to the just and righteous who fulfil thy will in Jerusalem which is above: O Lord of our death and our life, Father, Son and Holy Spirit for ever.

East Syrian Daily Office

God, we keep watch beside this dead person and pray
   for him.
His body is cold now and he is dead,
but we want to keep his name alive among us.
Yet we know that even this is impossible.
He will die in us too, his name will fade in our memory
   and even the sorrow that we feel now will be taken
   away from us.
We shall go on living without him.
We ask you, then, that he, living with you,
   may watch over us and intercede for us,
   that he may remind you unceasingly of our names
   as Jesus does,
a man near you in your eternity.

Huub Oosterhuis

Dead loved ones

But where are they, Lord, those I have loved?
Are they in ecstasy, taken up with holy loving in harmony
   with the Trinity?
Are they tormented in the night, burning with desire to love
   with an infinite love?
Are they in despair, condemned to their ownselves because
   they preferred themselves to others? Consumed with hate
   because they can no longer love?
Lord, my loved ones are near me.
I know that they live in the shadow.
My eyes can't see them because they have left for a moment
   their bodies as one leaves behind outmoded clothing.
Their souls deprived of their disguise, no longer communi-
   cate with me.

But in you, Lord, I hear them calling me.
I see them beckoning to me.
I hear them giving me advice.
For they are now more vividly present.
Before, our bodies touched but not our souls.
Now I meet them when I meet you.
I receive them when I receive you.
I love them when I love you.
O, my loved ones, eternally alive, who live in me,
Help me to learn thoroughly in this short life how to live
    eternally.
Lord, I love you, and I want to love you more.
It's you who make love eternal, and I want to love eternally.

Michel Quoist

Lord, help me to realise that love does not cease when we die. Surely those I love who have died still go on loving me as they come to live more fully and deeply with God? Yet, Lord, it is hard to understand. Our immediate loss makes us grieve, and forget that because of our union with you we are never separated from those who love you. It is hard—we are so taken up with the material world and so often forget the spiritual that we find it difficult to believe that because you live we will live also. The love that binds us to each other is very real when we have those we love with us, but when they die it isn't easy to believe love continues. Lord, give us faith to believe that we will never be separated from those who have died in your love. Deepen our relationship with you so that we may truly know in the depth of our being the joy of the communion of saints.

Help me to understand death, Lord. When friends die our intercourse seems to end abruptly. Do they simply cease to be? I believe that the living and the dead are all united in you. If this is so, can you give me a sense of their presence? Is perhaps the union with you and with others so deep, so hidden, that I cannot perceive it unless I pray deeply? Help me to understand the mystery of death which is so hard for the mind to grapple with, as hard as understanding your nearness and farness with us. Can these mysteries be only resolved by love and faith? If this is so, please Lord, give me more faith and deeper love.

'My soul is athirst for God, yea even for the living God': is this what the souls of the departed cry out when they see you, O my God? Here in this world our thirst for you is so mild our wills amble like little streams which do not know where they are going. Only the sight of you which our minds cannot imagine will give us a raging thirst that can only be quenched by your cool calm depths. Then our will to possess you wholly must become like a mighty river forging its way to the fullness of the ocean.

When I pray for the living I do not know their real needs, but when I pray for the dead I am sure that they can know neither rest nor peace till your light shines in the darkest corners of their souls and burns out all that is unworthy and impure. What more can I say to you on behalf of my dear dead, O Lord, than what your church has always said: 'Rest eternal grant to them and may light perpetual shine upon them'?

Colin Stephenson

After a death, for ourselves who are still living

Let us pray for ourselves,
who are severely tested by this death,
that we do not try to minimise this loss
or seek refuge from it in words,
and also that we do not brood over it
so that it overwhelms us
and isolates us from others.
May God grant us new courage
and confidence to face life.

Let us pray
for those who go on blindly,
unable to overcome their sorrow,
that they may be saved from their despair
for God's sake and for the sake of their dead
that God may be a fellow man for them
who can, in his silence comfort them
and bear their burden with them.

Let us pray
for those who have to go on living alone
after the death of their partner,
for those who mourn
the death of a child,
a friend or close relative
and all who have suffered
an unspeakable loss.

Huub Oosterhuis

For our nearest and dearest who are dead

O God, who knowest the necessities of all thy children,
we pray thee to have in thy holy keeping those precious

souls nearest and dearest to us, who have departed this life in thy fear and love. Provide for all their needs, sustain and comfort them, protect them, and grant them eternal joy in thy service. Give them peace and rest in thy presence, and bring them to that glorious perfection promised to thy saints; for the sake of him who died for us and rose again, thy Son, Jesus Christ our Lord.

from 'Burial Services' compiled by J. B. Bernadin

For us and our departed friends

O Lord our God, from whom neither life nor death can separate those who trust in thy love, and whose love holds in its embrace thy children in this world and in the next, so unite us to thyself that in fellowship with thee we may be always united to our loved ones whether here or there; give us courage, constancy and hope; through him who died and was buried and rose again for us, Jesus Christ our Lord.

William Temple (1881-1944)

For those whom we love

O Father of all, we pray thee for those whom we love but no longer see. Grant them thy peace; let light perpetual shine upon them and, in thy loving wisdom and almighty power, work in them the good purpose of thy perfect will, through Jesus Christ our Lord.

Scottish Prayer Book

O God, be with thy servants and handmaidens which have departed hence in the Lord, especially *N* and all others to whom our remembrance is due; Give them rest and peace in thy heavenly kingdom, and to us such a measure of communion with them as thou knowest to be best for us. And bring us all to serve thee in thy eternal kingdom, when thou wilt and as thou wilt, only without shame or sin; through Jesus Christ our Lord. Amen.

Lancelot Andrewes (1555-1626)

Let us give thanks to God for the fullness of *N's* life and the love which we have had for him. Jesus said: 'I am come that they might have life, and that they may have it more abundantly'. Let us rejoice in the knowledge that with him the treasure of *N's* life is not destroyed but fulfilled.

R. S. Ingamells

Death of an old man

I stood by his bed as he died, Lord, saying prayers and holding his hand. He was old and cantankerous, he was rude and he was lovable. After the struggling pain of the heart attack, he came to again, and calmed and then gently slipped away. He loved you, Lord, in his way, and he certainly prayed to you. He loved your mother too and prayed to her. So now grant him peace with you. Amen.

When someone I love has died

Lord, I am bewildered because *N* has died. Life with him about was wonderful. Somehow he transformed life and made it glorious. Now life seems empty and lonely. Help me to see that because we both love you, we are not separated, but because of you we are in some way still united. At the present moment this seems like wishful thinking, but you can make me perceive its reality. And help me to keep going when I am so shattered by grief.

Death of a husband

I pledged myself to him 'till death do us part'. It was a lovely time and then a hard grind. But through everything, Lord, I loved him for twenty years. And now you've taken him when he was still quite young. My heart is broken, Lord—I'm just flooding tears. Oh Lord, the agony! But why am I like this? Why can't I bear it sensibly and not make a fuss—I can't Lord—I loved him. Just let me go on loving him till I die too.

Lord, I do not understand why you have taken my husband to yourself. We were happy growing old together. Your action bewilders my simple faith; I am so lost and lonely now. Help and strengthen me. Give me a sense of your presence always with me, and help me to remember that my husband is safe in your keeping and that I am never separated from you and him even though I may not perceive this clearly. Increase my faith, dear Lord, and never leave me comfortless.

How awfully alone! He's dead: and I loved him: but I never knew how much I loved him till he was dead. Oh what a fool I've been. Oh, God, let us meet again in you.

When a husband or wife has died

Lord, I am so lonely since *N* has died. Weeping does not ease the pain. So many little things remind me of him and though I trust he is in your hands, I am overwhelmed by my loss. Help me to keep turning to you in faith. Comfort my loneliness in whatever way you think best. Above all give me courage to keep going.

Death of a son

I do miss my son so much, Lord. I loved cooking for him, mending his clothes and looking after him. I can't understand why you let him get killed so suddenly. He was hardly out of his teens. I am lost without him and don't sense his presence near me at all and I can't even visualise his being alive with you. There is an emptiness in my life. Show me how to live now, for it is very hard. I often think of your mother and how she must have felt after you had died on the cross. There must have been a dreadful gap in her life that even Saint John couldn't fill. Yet she had Saint John to look after. I wonder if it would ease my ache a little if you sent me someone else to look after. I'm an active person and not much good at thinking and praying deeply, and the pious advice of the holy is quite useless to me. Help me, Lord, in some way or the other for I am very miserable.

We pray, all loving Father, that you will comfort those who mourn. We pray especially for parents, relations and friends of *N*. Soothe them in their distress. Give them courage to face the world and go on living. In due time heal the wounds left by this death, and give us all faith to believe that in some way physical death is part of your divine purpose and leads to a more complete life. Through your Son who died but who rose again from the dead, Jesus Christ our Lord.

Marlborough College

Suicide

We had all felt and seen it coming, Lord. She was so deeply sad, depressed beyond all human endurance. The doctors tried drugs and her friends laughter and firmness, patience and love. But she could not pull out of it. And so she took that overdose and died. Well, Lord, I feel in my heart that you could have boundless love and care and compassion for her and that now she will never more be depressed, but know the fullness of joy and peace in you. So thus I pray in confidence, Lord.

When a friend commits suicide

Lord, we cannot understand why *N* took his own life. You alone know what he suffered. Forgive our lack of understanding, and give him the comfort and compassion which we so unthinkingly failed to give. Lord, we pray that he may rest in peace with you in the warmth of your love; and, Lord, give support to his family and those close to him through your healing and redeeming love which you showed us in your Son.

When a baby has died

O God, our heavenly Father, whose ways are hidden and thy works wonderful, comfort, we pray thee, this woman and her husband whose hearts are heavy with sorrow. Surround them with thy protection, and grant them grace to face the future with good courage and hope. Teach them to use this pain in deeper sympathy for all who suffer, so that they may share in thy work of turning sorrow into joy; through Jesus Christ our Lord.

Guild of Health

My mother's death

Lord, when someone close to us dies suddenly, it is shattering in a dramatic way and for a time we are paralysed with grief. But later, when life has started again, little things remind us of the dead—my mother's sewing, the dress she looked so nice in. I can't bring myself to give them away even though they constantly remind me that I won't see her again. Lord, it is hard to accept that death is such a sharp break; and we cannot visualise what life with you after death will be like. Lord, deaden my distress and make me realise more clearly that we are all united, both live and dead in you.

On the death of an animal

I've always loved my cat so much and now, Lord, he's dead. Perhaps you'd like me to be a bit more interested in other things or people, but his company has meant so much in my lonely life. He really seemed to care when others forgot or could not be bothered. Now he's gone, and I am so very much alone. Thank you for making animals, Lord, and for allowing us to have them. Can you teach me to love more through them?

For those who mourn

Let the cry of widows, orphans and destitute children enter into thine ears, O most loving Saviour. Comfort them with a mother's tenderness, shield them from the perils of this world, and bring them at last to thy heavenly home.

John Cosin (1595-1672)

216

Heavenly Father, hear our voice out of the deep sorrow which thou in thy mysterious wisdom hast brought upon us. We know that thou art with us, and that whatsoever cometh is a revelation of thine unchanging love. Thou knowest what is best for us. Thy will be done. Thou gavest and thou hast taken away, blessed be thy name. O keep our souls from all the temptations of this hour of mourning, that we may neither sorrow as those without hope, nor lose our trust in thee; but that the darker this earthly scene comes the lighter may be our vision of that eternal world where all live before thee. And grant that the remnant of this our family, O Lord, still being upon earth, may be steadfast in faith, joyful through hope, and rooted in love, and so may pass the waves of this troublesome world, that finally we may come to the land of everlasting life, there to reign with thee, world without end; through Jesus Christ our Lord.

Laurence R. Tuttiett (1825-1897)

Almighty God, Father of all mercies and giver of all comfort, deal graciously, we pray thee, with all who mourn the loss of those dear to them; that casting every care on thee, they may know the consolation of thy love, through Jesus Christ our Lord.

O heavenly Father, whose blessed Son Jesus Christ did weep at the grave of Lazarus, his friend, look, we beseech thee, with compassion upon those who are now in sorrow and affliction; comfort them, O Lord, with thy gracious consolations; make them to know that all things work together for good to them that love thee; and grant them evermore sure trust and confidence in thy fatherly care; through Jesus Christ our Lord.

Scottish Prayer Book

Comfort in grief

O God, whose blessed Son on the cross did know the desolation of loneliness from thee; comfort these thy servants in their grief and emptiness, enfold them in the arms of thy mercy and give them peace; through Jesus Christ our Lord.

Robert N. Rodenmayer

The saints who have gone before

O king eternal, immortal, invisible, who in the righteousness of thy saints hast given us an example of godly life, and in their blessedness a sure pledge of the hope of our calling; grant, we beseech thee, that being compassed about with so great a cloud of witnesses, we may run with patience the race that is set before us, and with them receive the crown of glory that fadeth not away; through Jesus Christ our Lord.

Acts of Devotion

Heaven

Bring us, O Lord God, at our last awakening into the house and gate of heaven, to enter into that gate and dwell in that house, where there shall be no darkness nor dazzling, but one equal light; no voice nor silence, but one equal music; no fears nor hopes, but one equal possession; no ends nor beginnings, but one equal eternity; in the habitation of thy glory and dominion, world without end.

After John Donne (1573-1631), derived from a sermon by E. Milner-White and Briggs

Before visiting the bereaved

Lord, teach me what to say when I go to visit those who have just been bereaved. I feel utterly powerless in the face of their grief. They have to suffer so much. I am distressed for them, but words seem to fail me. Act through me, and make me the instrument of your comfort even if I say very little. Give me understanding compassion and give them faith in your strength, and peace so as to be able to endure their pain and loneliness which is so very deep. O help of the helpless, help us all in our distress for the sake of your Son who knew the depths of human suffering.

I can't imagine, Lord, standing with your mother at the foot of the cross, looking up at you dying there and saying: 'Don't worry God loves him so, it's all in his plan. We must accept his will'. I suppose in hindsight I could say that this might have been the thing to say—but when it was happening —what should I have said then? I ask you, Lord, because I'm knotted up and tongue-tied at the grief of mothers who lose their sons, husbands their wives. Even though I believe in eternal life and your love and your care, how can this come through now, sitting beside a bed of pain, identifying a smashed body in a mortuary? Perhaps I can only be there, and believe and love on, despite the horror and pain, through it all. Help me to be there silent or in the right way.

O thou in whose house are many mansions, speak through me to those whose loved one has gone from their sight, but not from thine. There is nothing in me to heal the wounded heart or fill the aching void. But let thy words of comfort and truth be given to me to speak that these sorrowing ones may find their peace in thee; through Jesus Christ our Lord.

Prayers for the Minister's Day

COMFORTING AND STRENGTHENING PRAYERS

Though I walk through the valley of the shadow of death,
I will fear no evil, for thou art with me.

Psalm 23.4

We would be less than human if we did not look round
for help and comfort from one source or another when we
find ourselves in trouble, suffering or dying. The Psalmist
says: 'A brother helping a brother is like a strong fortress'.
Or more recently in history the English poet has used those
often quoted words: 'No man is an island, himself alone'.

For this reason, we have another section of this book
which offers suggestions for 'suffering with others', so that
the more fortunate may offer themselves in prayer, presence
or material aid to those who are worse off than themselves.

This present section is specifically for those who are
suffering, because we know from experience the great
additional comfort and strength which can be derived
beyond the human touch and in the whole realm of the
spiritual. There may well be some who have not been able to
penetrate the veil, and have found no comfort anywhere. If
such a person reads this page, we say; 'Take courage,
persevere; do not despair; as best you can keep on turning to
God, however unknown or even unbelieved he may be. This
is truly the "shade of his hand, outstretched caressingly".'

Be thou my stronghold, whereunto I may always resort:
thou hast promised to help me, for thou art my house of
defence and my castle.

Deliver me, O my God, out of the hand of the ungodly;
out of the hand of the unrighteous and cruel man.

For thou, O Lord God, art the thing that I long for; thou art my hope, even from my youth.

Cast me not away in the time of age: forsake me not when my strength faileth me.

Go not far from me, O God: my God, haste thee to help me.

Psalm 71

By your example help us when we are afraid and strengthen us.

Lord Jesus Christ:
    Who in the days of thy flesh
    Didst steadfastly set thy face
    To go to Jerusalem;
    Didst suffer the agony in the garden,
    And dereliction of the cross . . .

    Who yet, for the joy that was set before thee,
    Didst endure the cross,
    Despising the shame,
    And art set down
    At the right hand of God:

Strengthen us:
    When we shrink from unknown ways,
    Hold us firmly when we are afraid;
    Help us to follow thee without swerving,
    To the end;
    Out of weakness, make us strong;
    Lighten our darkness,
    And beat down Satan under our feet;
    And finally bring us unto everlasting life.

Anonymous

For peace when worried

Lord, by thy divine silence, by thy wondrous patience, by thine adorable humility, keep me quiet and still, and possess me with thy peace.

Father Andrew

Hear my prayer, O Lord;
give ear to my supplications!
In thy faithfulness answer me,
in thy righteousness!
For the enemy has pursued me;
he has crushed my life to the ground;
he has made me to sit in darkness like those long dead.
Therefore my spirit faints within me;
my heart within me is appalled.
I stretch out my hands to thee;
my soul thirsts for thee like a parched land.
Make haste to answer me, O Lord!
My spirit fails!
Hide not thy face from me,
lest I be like unto those who go down into the pit.
Let me hear in the morning of thy steadfast love,
for in thee I put my trust.
Teach me the way I should go,
for to thee I lift up my soul.
Deliver me, O Lord, from my enemies!
I have fled to thee for refuge!
Teach me to do thy will,
for thou art my God!
Let thy good spirit lead me
on a level path!
For thy name's sake, O Lord, preserve my life!
In thy righteousness bring me out of trouble!

Psalm 143

Lord, when I am tired and everything is going wrong, it is wonderful to let go and let you take over. By leaving my helplessness to your strength, I forget myself and there is peace in a deep way. Strengthen me so I will not forget you when you make me go out into the hurly burly of life again.

Grant unto us, almighty God, in all time of sore distress, the comfort of the forgiveness of our sins. In time of darkness give us blessed hope, in time of sickness of body give us quiet courage; and when the heart is bowed down, and the soul is very heavy, and life is a burden, and pleasure a weariness, and the sun is too bright, and life too mirthful, then may that Spirit, the Spirit of the Comforter, come upon us, and after our darkness may there be the clear shining of the heavenly light; that so, being uplifted again by thy mercy, we may pass on through this our mortal life with quiet courage, patient hope, and unshaken trust, hoping through thy loving-kindness and tender mercy to be delivered from death into the large life of the eternal years. Hear us of thy mercy, through Jesus Christ our Lord. Amen.

George Dawson (1821-1876)

But now that great anguish has left me; it came like a blinding flash of light that Christ did not resist evil, that he allowed himself to be violently done to death, that he knew that the exquisite delicacy and loveliness of the merest detail of the Christian life would survive the Passion; that indeed, far from being destroyed by it, it depended on it. And so it is now; that which is holy and tender and beautiful, will not be swept away or destroyed by war; on the contrary, we can still say: 'Ought not Christ to suffer these things and so enter into his glory'.

Anonymous

I walk among shadows
O liege Lord,
my love,
shadows
of your bright glory!

Anonymous

I take great comfort in watching you, Lord, when you are
with sinners. I get myself lost in wrongness and self and
almost despair in my weakness. But when I read about you
with the woman at the well, or with the woman taken in
adultery—you with Peter, you even with Judas—then
though I feel hopelessly cut off from you and blank about
you; still I know how gently healing you have been to men
and women in your time, and I pray: Give me comfort and
raise me up and give me hope. Amen.

Fear-not for I am with you, be not dismayed for I am
your God. I will strengthen you and will uphold you with
my right hand.

After Isaiah

Like the deer that thirsts for water,
O God, I long for you.
Weeping, I have heard them taunt me:
'What help is in your God?'

Gladly I would lead your people,
rejoicing to your house.
Trust in God, my soul and praise him,
and he will dry your tears.

Grief and pain, like roaring torrents,
had swept my soul away.
But his mercy is my rescue,
I praise him all my days.

Weeping, I have heard them taunt me:
'What help is in your God?'
Rock of strength, do not forget me,
In you alone I trust.

To the Father praise and honour,
all glory to the Son,
honour to the Holy Spirit;
let God be glorified.

*Psalm 41 paraphrased
by Luke Connaughton and Kevin Mayhew*

Courage

Courage is a nebulous quality, Lord, giving an extra
   dimension to a man.
Its presence or its absence is only seen as the lions
   approach, as the door of the den is sealed.
This measure of strength is the measure of your indwelling
   Spirit.
You radiate strength from the cross.
Share your resources, Lord.
Share them with all who are persecuted for holding to
   their integrity.
Share them also with me.
Let the lions always fail.

Rex Chapman

Help us with the grace of courage that we be none of us
cast down. When we sit lamenting amid the ruins of our

happiness or our integrity, touch us with fire from the altar that we may be up and doing to rebuild our city.

R. L. Stevenson (1850-1894)

Lord Christ, you accepted the gift of life in faith, and lived it out with courage. You were able to walk the narrow path, withstand temptation's power, and hold fast even at the time of dereliction. Surely, you can speak as no other in this anxious age, and teach us all that courage comes in waiting patiently upon the Father. Please give us that strong courage; for are you not with us wherever we must go?

Please be with those who are lost, who simply do not know what they believe, and show them where they stand.

Please be with the anxious, who begin to despair even of life itself, and show them meaning.

Please be with those who are brought to the test, who feel tensions which rack the mind, and show them how to take one step in obedience and trust.

Please be with the sick, who are held back from the life they would live, and give them hope and perfect healing.

Please be with those who do wrong, who steal and murder and destroy, and bring them through repentance to a new way of looking at things.

Please be with the bereaved, who are face to face with the grim reality of death, and give them the generosity of spirit to entrust their lost ones to your living care.

Please be with all people who must live out their lives facing challenge as it comes, and speak strong words of courage to their troubled minds, that they may finish their course.

Through Jesus Christ, our Lord.

Contemporary Prayers for Public Worship

O most merciful Lord, we beseech thee that thou wilt give courage to thy soldiers, wisdom to the perplexed, endurance to sufferers, fresh vigour and interest in life to those who have lost heart, a sense of thy presence to the lonely, and bless and prosper all of this household, for the sake of Jesus Christ.

Arthur H. O. McCheane (19th century)

My Lord God, give me once more the courage to hope; merciful God, let me hope once again, fructify my barren and infertile mind.

Sören Kierkegaard (1813-1855)

Blessed Lord, who wast tempted in all things like as we are, have mercy on our frailty. Out of weakness give us strength. Grant to us thy fear that we may fear thee only. Support us in time of temptation. Embolden us in time of danger. Help us to do thy work with good courage, and to continue thy faithful soldiers and servants unto our life's end through Jesu Christ our Lord.

Brooke F. Westcott (1825-1901)

Take to thyself all my poverty and need

O thou who hast willed to be called Charity, give me charity, that I may love thee more than I love myself, and care not at all what I do with myself, so long as I am doing what is pleasing in thy sight. Grant me, O Father, though I dare not always call myself thy child, at least to be thy faithful little servant and the sheep of thy pasture. Speak to thy servant's heart sometimes so that thy consolations may give joy to my soul. And teach me to speak to thee often in prayer. Take to thyself all my poverty and need, O Lord, my God and my Father. Have pity on my weakness, O my strength; and may it be to thy great glory that my feebleness continues to serve thee.

William of Saint Thierry (1085-1148)

In God is my hope

For God alone my soul waits in silence,
    for my hope is from him.
He only is my rock and my salvation,
    my fortress; I shall not be shaken.
On God rests my deliverance and my honour;
    my mighty rock, my refuge is God.
Trust in him at all times, O people;
    pour out your heart before him;
God is a refuge for us.

Psalm 62

When things are hopeless

When things are completely hopeless, I leave all to you and live in the present moment. In the darkness there is peace because I am trusting you so much more than I usually do. You have taken away all the props and supports of my life, and left me only yourself. The loss of them hurts and aches, but the gift of yourself, though frightening and demanding, is so much more than my human supports. Help me to adapt to having you as my all; stop me from wanting lesser things instead because they are easier to understand and cope with. I am very afraid to fall into your hands completely—it may be so very dark and so very burning.

For hope in adversity; the fiery furnace (Daniel 3)

You are the Lord of fire
Present in the fiery furnace,
Present in the heat of life,
Present in situations of horror and despair,
Present in the prisons that incarcerate men for their
  beliefs.
Shadrach, Meshach and Abednego were lucky ones, Lord.
They came out unscathed.
Not all are so lucky,
Not all understand the tyrannies of life and remain
  unharmed.
You are with men in their suffering, in their aloneness
  and ignominy and death.
Be with them.
Be with them through us who are your limbs.
Give us a glimmering of hope in hopeless situations;
For where there is no hope there is nothing.

Rex Chapman

Thanksgiving after adversity

O Lord, my God, I cried to you in my trouble and you
heard me; I put my trust in you and have not been confounded. You have turned my heaviness into joy, and guided
me with gladness. Therefore I praise you with all my heart,
and give thanks to your holy name for ever. Hear me and
accept me, for the sake of Jesus Christ our Lord.

L. Tuttiett (1825-1897)

Protection of God

Eternal Father, men have always looked to you for protection. They have thought of you as a cave to hide in, a harbour to make for, a fort to retreat to. They have thought of you as men think of home, as the place where they ought to be safe, where there is friendship and security.

We thank you that we too can think of you like this, so that we need not pretend, but can admit how weak and frightened life sometimes makes us feel.

Yet we realise we can be over-protected. This can make us lazy; it can keep us weak. So we ask you to help us accept that life is hazardous, learning from Jesus that its chances and dangers have a place in your purpose.

More Contemporary Prayers

God's love for us was revealed
when God sent into the world his only Son
so that we could have life through him;
this is the love I mean:
not our love for God,
but God's love for us when he sent his Son
to be the sacrifice that takes our sins away.

1 John 4. 9-10

Christ did not say: 'Thou shalt not be tempted, thou shalt not be travailed, thou shalt not be afflicted'; but he did say: 'Thou shalt not be overcome'. God wills that we take heed of these words, and that we be ever strong in sure trust, in weal or woe. For he loves and likes us, and so wills he that we love and like him, and mightily trust in him; and all shall be well.

Lady Julian of Norwich (1342-c.1412)

Tranquillity

Lord Jesus, by thine own peace of soul,
   rooted and living in the eternal Father,
   serene in the hours of commotion and anguish,
   grant me thy tranquillity.
Be my life hid in thine;
   let thy fearless and imperturbable Spirit
   come to dwell in mine.

Thou hast said: 'I will give you rest':
   thy presence is our peace.
Thy Spirit is the donor of every good grace,
   and, in all that he bestows, brings with him
   thine eternal purpose, thy divine counsel,
   thy support and most ready help,
   thy courage and thy victory,
   thy love.
Whom then, what then, shall I fear?

Whom then, what then, shall I fear?
   thou who guidest us in the calm
   wilt not leave us in the storm.

So let me be still; and inwardly worship,
   in private, in public, everywhere, always,
   and know that thou art God,
   my God, God with me.
Be thou the rock of my repose,
   the moving pillar before and behind my pilgrimage;
   not as the world gives,
   giving thy peace.

Eric Milner-White

Lord, I cannot find words to express my joy and thanks
for your revelation to me. I have always known that you

love me, but I have never experienced the radiation of your love for me so intensely. I have been trying to open myself to you in every way I could. I have loved you in people, in the Eucharist, in prayer and now at Christmas time at the crib. I did not know that your love for me could be so indescribably beautiful, so personal, and so powerful. It seems to take my inadequate love and make it more like yours. Lord, with the strength of your love I will love others more humbly and understandingly. In times of doubt and worry, and when I am tired, the remembrance of the warmth of the power and radiation of your love will sustain me, O Lord, my strength and support.

The Lord bless us and keep us!
The Lord let his face shine upon us
and be gracious to us!
The Lord look upon us kindly and give us peace.

For thine is the kingdom,
the power and the glory,
for ever and ever. Amen.

RESURRECTION

I am the resurrection ... Do you believe this?

John 11. 25–26

The whole course of this book, from the claim of Christ that he will draw all men to himself if he is lifted up, through to his promise of paradise to the good thief on the cross, is underlining the continuing life of Jesus now and forever ... and his promise: 'I am the resurrection. If anyone believes in me, even though he dies he will live, and whoever lives and believes in me will never die.' (*John 11. 25–26*)

This is basic Christianity. But Christ had to ask Martha, to whom he was talking at the time: 'Do you believe this?' (*John 11. 26*) She was standing shocked and sad at the tomb of her brother, who may well have died young. Her response was: 'Yes, Lord, I believe you are the Christ, the Son of God'. (*John 11. 27*)

When we are faced by the death of someone we love, we are likely to be overcome with natural and good human emotion. But this can prevent us from living through and accepting that which is somewhere at the back of the mind, though it may never have had a 'guts' acceptance ... namely life after death, resurrection.

What we would urge you to do, if you are reading this book of thoughts and prayers, is to take some time to think deeply about resurrection—here and hereafter—to read about it, to pray about it, and above all to steep yourself in what we can only describe as a 'resurrection mentality' or life.

Please take this personally and seriously. Here lies the truest comfort, because it is the truth, and because we can then learn to pray truthfully from the heart the prayer of Thomas More that 'we may all meet merrily in heaven'.

This will depend almost entirely on the genuine depth of prayer-relationship with God in Christ. We cannot love or trust unless we know, unless we grow in relationship with God who is life and love.

Anyone can say this, but it must be lived. You must discover for yourself the truth; you must be able to say in answer to Christ's question: 'Yes, Lord' . . . meaning it with all your heart, soul, mind and strength. Then we can assure you that you will, despite pain or anxiety, through sickness and into death itself grow in that peace which passes all understanding . . . passes it because it survives against what seem, humanly speaking, to be impossible odds, to a depth of serenity, joy and love which has to be either seen or experienced to be believed. This is the triumph of the cross on the limbs of which is stretched in love and life-bearing death the One who said: 'Come to me all you who labour and are heavy burdened and I will give you rest'.

To this our fearless reply should be: Come, Lord Jesus.

And death shall have no dominion.
Dead men naked they shall be one
With the man in the wind and the west moon;
When their bones are picked clean and clean bones are
    gone,
They shall have stars at elbow and foot;
Though they go mad they shall be sane,
Though they sink through the sea they shall rise again;
Though loves be lost love shall not;
And death shall have no dominion.

And death shall have no dominion,
Under the windings of the sea;
They lying long shall not die windily;
Twisting in racks when sinews give way,

Strapped to a wheel, yet they shall not break;
Faith in their hands shall snap in two,
And the unicorn evils run them through;
Split all ends up they shan't crack;
And death shall have no dominion.

And death shall have no dominion.
No more may gulls cry at their ears
Or waves break loud on the sea shores;
Where blew a flower may a flower go and
Lift its head to the blows of the rain;
Though they be mad and dead as nails,
Heads of the characters hammer through the daisies;
Break in the sun till the sun breaks down,
And death shall have no dominion.

Dylan Thomas

Do you not know that all of us who have been baptised
into Christ Jesus were baptised into his death?

We were buried therefore with him by baptism into death,
so that as Christ was raised from the dead by the glory of the
Father, we too might walk in newness of life.

But if we have died with Christ, we believe that we shall
also live with him. For we know that Christ being raised
from the dead will never die again; death no longer has
dominion over him. The death he died he died to sin, once
for all, but the life he lives he lives to God. So also you must
consider yourselves dead to sin and alive to God in Christ
Jesus.

Romans 6. 3–4, 8–11

Stephen, filled with the Holy Spirit, gazed into heaven
and saw the glory of God, and Jesus standing at God's
right hand. 'I can see heaven thrown open', he said, 'and
the Son of man standing at the right hand of God.'

Acts 7. 55–56

God's love for us was revealed
when God sent into the world his only Son
so that we could have life through him;
this is the love I mean:
not our love for God,
but God's love for us when he sent his Son
to be the sacrifice that takes our sins away.

1 John 4. 9–10

Because I live, ye shall live also.

John 14. 19

For I am persuaded that neither death, nor life, nor principalities or powers . . . nor height, nor depth, nor any other creature, shall be able to separate us from the love of God, which is in Christ Jesus our Lord.

Romans 38. 39

Blessed be you, O God and Father of our Lord Jesus Christ by whose great mercy we have been born again to a living hope through the resurrection of Jesus Christ from the dead to an inheritance that is imperishable, undefiled and unfading reserved in heaven for us. Keep us, O God, by your power unto salvation through our Lord Jesus Christ, whom not having seen we love and in whom we believe and rejoice with unutterable joy. Amen.

After 1 Peter 1

The Lord is risen!
He is risen indeed!
Alleluia!
Lord Jesus, we greet you, risen from the dead.
We thought your way of love was a dead end, leading only to the cross, now we see that it is a way of life.
We thought your whole life was wasted: now we know that it was gloriously worthwhile.
We thought your suffering was pointless: now we can see God's purpose in it.
We thought that death was the end of you: now we know that your life was too great to be ended by death.
Lord Jesus, we greet you, risen from the dead.

More Contemporary Prayers

I adore and praise and bless thee, O Lord, Jesus Christ, giving thanks for the love and confidence with which having overcome death, rising from the tomb thou hast glorified our human flesh; and, ascending into heaven, hast placed it at the right hand of God; beseeching thee on behalf of the souls for which I pray, that thou wilt deign to make them partakers of thy glory and thy victory.

The True Prayers of Saint Gertrude (1256-c. 1302) and Saint Mechthild (c. 1210-1289)

Dying you destroyed our death,
rising you restored our life.
Lord Jesus, come in glory.
By your cross and resurrection
you have set us free.
You are the saviour of the world.

Roman Acclamations

You are more than alive—you are Lord.

Acts 1. 1–11

You are not only risen and alive, you are Lord.
This your ascension, your ascendency over the whole
    universe.
You stand over and above all that is best in life as its
    source.
You stand above all that is worst as ultimate victor.
You stand above all powers and authorities as judge.
You stand above all failure and weakness and sin as
    forgiveness and love.
You alone are worthy of total allegiance, total
    commitment.
You are Lord,
'My Lord and my God'.

Rex Chapman

'Christ, the Lord is risen today',
Sons of men and angels say;
Raise your joys and triumphs high,
Sing, ye heavens, and earth, reply.
Love's redeeming work is done,
Fought the fight the battle won;
Lo! our Sun's eclipse is o'er;
Lo! He sets in blood no more.

Vain the stone, the watch, the seal;
Christ has burst the gates of hell:
Death in vain forbids his rise;
Christ has opened Paradise.
Lives again our glorious king;
Where, O Death, is now thy sting?
Once he died, our souls to save;
Where thy victory, O grave?

Soar we now where Christ has led,
Following our exalted Head;
Made like him, like him we rise;
Ours the cross, the grave, the skies.
Hail the Lord of earth and heaven!
Praise by thee by both be given;
Thee we greet triumphant now;
Hail the Resurrection thou!

Charles Wesley (1707–1788)

O Christ, whose wondrous birth meanest nothing unless
we be born again, whose death and sacrifice nothing if thou
be risen alone: raise up and exalt us, O Saviour, both
now to the estate of grace and hereafter to the seat of glory;
where with the Father and the Holy Spirit thou livest and
reignest, God for ever and ever.

Eric Milner-White

For a joyful resurrection

O heavenly Father, whose blessed Son has 'risen from the
dead, and become the first fruits of them that slept', grant
that we may so live and die in him that when he shall appear
again in his glory we may rise to everlasting life. We pray
also for all our brethren in Christ, especially our relations
and friends, and neighbours, that we may all share in a
joyful resurrection, and be partakers of thy heavenly
kingdom, through Jesus Christ our Lord.

W. Walsham How (1823-1897)

Almighty God, who didst raise from the dead our Lord Jesus Christ and didst set him at thy right hand in the glory everlasting, I thank thee for this hope of immortality with which through many ages thou hast cheered and enlightened the souls of thy saints, and which thou didst most surely seal through the same Jesus Christ our Lord.

John Bailey

i thank You God for most this amazing
day: for the leaping greenly spirits of trees
and a blue true dream of sky; and for everything
which is natural which is infinite which is yes

(i who have died am alive again today,
and this is the sun's birthday; this is the birth
day of life and of love and wings: and of the gay
great happening illimitably earth)

how should tasting touching hearing seeing
breathing any—lifted from from the no
of all nothing—human merely being
doubt unimaginable You?

(now the ears of my ears awake and
now the eyes of my eyes are opened)

e. e. cummings

O risen and victorious Christ, whose power and love destroyed the darkness and death of sin; ascend, we pray thee, the throne of our hearts, and so rule our wills by the might of that immortality wherewith thou hast set us free, that we may evermore be alive unto God, through the power of thy glorious resurrection, world without end.

John W. Suter

Heavenly Father, Jesus has broken out of the tomb and gone ahead of us into the world, but we try to lock him in our churches, to display him to outsiders as we think fit; or to take him on our pious excursions as if he belonged to us. How pathetic! How futile! Please forgive our condescension, and end our conceit. Through Jesus Christ our Lord.

More Contemporary Prayers

O thou God and Father of our Lord Jesus Christ, we render thee most humble and hearty thanks that thou didst raise thine only begotten Son from the dead and set him at thine right hand in the heavenly places. Grant us grace, we beseech thee, to apprehend with true faith the glorious mystery of our Saviour's resurrection, and fill our hearts with joy and a lively hope, that amid all the sorrows, trials and temptations of our mortal state, and in the hour of death, we may derive strength and comfort from this sure pledge of an inheritance incorruptible and undefiled and that fadeth not away; through Jesus Christ our Lord.

Prayers for Family Worship

We give thee thanks, almighty Father, who hast delivered us from the power of darkness, and translated us into the kingdom of thy Son; grant, we beseech thee, that as by his death he has restored to us hope and peace, he may raise us up with him to life eternal through the same Jesus Christ our Lord.

From the Mozarabic

Pour upon us, O Lord, thy heavenly benediction, that we may be armed with the faith of the resurrection so as not to fear any army of men sent against us.

Mathew Parker (1504-1575)

Lord who have died and risen again, touch our hearts so that we, with the help of your Holy Spirit, may be drawn to love you with our whole being. Give us a continual vision of your risen glory so that when we are surrounded by the cares of daily life, and are tempted to rush off after others and other things as substitutes for you, we may realise that you are what our hearts are seeking. When our lives are full of pain and suffering help us to remember that you endured the passion and the cross knowing that you were doing the will of your Father and by going through with it you were raised to glory, and show us that glory will be the end of our suffering too if we trust you. Always let us see that you are the end of our desiring and that it is only with you that our restless hearts will rest peacefully.

The wounds you received on the cross your disciples recognised in the resurrection. Should I not learn a lesson here? It seems natural that I should shrink from being wounded, as you did at Gethsemane. But also I need to recognise that you accepted all that was to come, and did not run away. Can you teach me, Lord? Can I learn to greet

242

pain and sorrow, all the natural twists of life with equanimity; and to live through life so that everything is part of development towards resurrection, most of all death itself? Can you teach me and can I learn that a demand of future glory is the right living of the problem of pain now? I'll try to learn if you teach me, Lord.

Lord, come alive within my experience,
>within my sorrows and disappointments and doubts,
>within the ordinary movements of my life.
Come alive as the peace and joy and assurance that is
>stronger than the locked doors within, with which we
>try to shut out life.
Come alive as the peace and joy and assurance that
>nothing in life or death can kill.

Rex Chapman

O Lord, I see resurrection is bound in with love; you were raised because you died in love; I am raised when, in love, I die to myself. Resurrection gives a new colour to living; the glow of dawn touches my heart and gives me hope and transforms all things and all my relationships with others. It brings hope too that I will know you in the sun in paradise. The last dying will bring me to you, the everlasting love and light.

Hereafter—peace

There shall be no sorrow, no pain, no complaint, no fear, no death. There is no malice to rise against us; no misery to afflict us; no hunger, thirst, weariness, temptation to disquiet us. There, O there, one day is better than a thousand; there is rest from our labours, peace from our enemies, freedom from our sins. How many clouds of discontentment darken the sunshine of our joy, while we are here below! Complaint of evils, past sense of present, fear of future, have shared our lives amongst them. There shall we be 'always joyful, always satisfied', with the vision of that God, in whose presence there is fulness of joy, and at whose right hand are pleasures for evermore.

What stick we at, my beloved? Is there a heaven, or is there none? Have we a Saviour there, or have we none? We know there is a heaven as sure as that there is an earth below us: we know we have a Saviour there, as sure as there are men that we converse with upon earth we know there is happiness, as sure as we know there is misery and mutability upon earth. O, our miserable sottishness and infidelity; if we do not contemn the best offers of the world, and lifting up our eyes and hearts to heaven, say: 'It is good to be here!' Even so, Lord Jesus, come quickly. To Him, that hath purchased and prepared this glory for us, together with the Father and Blessed Spirit, one incomprehensible God, be all praise for ever. Amen.

Joseph Hall (1574–1656)

Send your risen power into the Church

O Christ, our Lord, whose resurrection did turn thy timid disciples into men of courage and daring: let thy risen power come upon thy church that she may proclaim thy saving principles to the world. Grant her such a love of the souls of men that she may draw all men into thy family and so in union with thee, who with the Father and Holy Spirit art our God for ever and ever.

George Appleton

Meeting the risen Christ

Once Lord, I went from Jerusalem to Emmaus on a glorious Easter day. I took part in the breaking of bread at Emmaus, and in a small, deep way, I knew you in the breaking of bread. I suppose since then I have understood a little better that my eyes were covered, that I was looking for you in the wrong way, in the wrong place. Now I thank you that, not always but often, I sense your new life in the world, I meet you on the way and I know in myself I must be joined in sharing your life: 'Was it not right that Christ should suffer these things and to enter into his glory?' Let me share, Lord.

Resurrection now

What I'm asking, Lord, is that I may have resurrection now. I don't mean die physically and rise again, though if this is your will for me I'll try to say 'yes', but I mean spiritually. I mean a new resurrection through a new baptism in your Spirit. I mean seeing things differently, recognising you and people and life itself in a new way. I mean coming alive in you and sloughing off all the deadness that covers my inward vision. This I call resurrection now, Lord, and I ask for it that I may live newly now and so later live eternally. Amen.

Lord, Mary Magdalen found the empty tomb frightening and disturbing when she saw your body was no longer there, but then you showed yourself to her in your resurrection body and her despair was changed into joy. Lord, so often when I do not find you where I expect to, I get panicky. It is so easy to forget that you are risen, glorious, and vital as light, and can be met with in the most unexpected places if we look for you with open, loving, and un-self-clouded eyes.

Lord, help me to remember we too are raised with you and our lives are glorious and full of unexpectedness because you are with us; stop us from returning to the seeming safety of the tomb to find you in the form we want you to have. Make us joyous and unafraid of life and death for you are Lord of both.

Lord, I believe . . .

I think I have said again and again and again with my lips that I believe in the resurrection and life everlasting. But now I think, Lord, it was only with my lips. I fear it was, because in time of illness or distress, it all fades and becomes unreal. I am not sure how I go about it, but of one thing I am sure, and that is that I am going to chase that belief, let myself seep in it and it into me, so that my whole being is saturated. Then I am confident I will believe again, more truly and more deeply . . . that I shall come alive in the present with a resurrection of spirit and depth, and that this will spill over and swamp death, swallowing it up in new life.

EPILOGUE

The old saying tells us:

As a tree falls, so shall it lie;
As a man lives, so shall he die.

It is interesting and moving that those astronauts who first closely viewed the moon have come back with an intensified awareness of the 'good Earth'. We who live permanently on Earth miss so much of its beauty, of its fragile and brilliant balance of nature, of its supreme disaster and supreme masterpiece—man.

We who have compiled this book and those whose works we have included, belong to a vast body of believers. Not by any means all believers are Christians; indeed there are many who 'believe' but belong to no church or sect and would deny that they are in any way 'religious'. Yet somehow they accept with us (vaguely, doubtfully, questioningly or with deep certainty) that Earth and man are God's creation.

Further, we accept the line from the Letter to the Hebrews: There is no eternal city for us in this life but we look for one in the life to come. (*Hebrews 13.14*)

That is the reason why we would draw your attention to that other line, this time from the Letter to the Romans: Faith leads to faith—or as scripture says 'The upright man finds life through faith'. (*Romans 1.17*)

If you will only live by faith, you will die in faith. The living atmosphere of faith finds fulfilment in three joyful promises of Jesus Christ:

Come to me all you who labour and are overburdened and I will give you rest. (*Matthew 11.28*)

I have come so that they may have life and have it to the full. (*John 10.10*)

Anyone who follows me will not be walking in the dark:
he will have the light of life. (*John 8.12*)

Finally, therefore, we can only encourage you to listen
and to live with the words of the last chapter of Revelation:

'Come!' say the Spirit and the bride.

'Come!' let each hearer reply.

Come forward, you who are thirsty; accept the water
of life, a free gift to all who desire it.

INDEX OF SUBJECTS

251

252

INDEX OF AUTHORS AND SOURCES

ACKNOWLEDGMENTS

The authors and publishers wish to express their gratitude to the following for permission to include copyright material in this book:

Gill and Macmillan for the extracts from *Prayers of Life* by Michel Quoist.

SPCK for the extracts from *Christian Priest Today* by Michael Ramsey, *Pray and Live* by A. D. Duncan, *My God, My Glory* by Eric Milner-White, *Lord, I believe* by Austin Farrer.

Faber and Faber for the poem 'The moon was caught in the branches' from *Markings* by Dag Hammarskjöld and the extract from *Fortitude and Temperance* by Josef Pieper.

Paulist/Newman Press for the extracts from *Your Word is Near* by Huub Oosterhuis.

BBC Publications for the prayer from *New Every Morning*.

William Heineman for the prayer from *Are You Running with Me, Jesus?* by Malcolm Boyd.

Mrs William Temple for the prayer by the late Archbishop Temple.

Oxford University Press for the extract from 'Ecce Homo' from *Collected Poems* by David Gascoyne and the prayer from *A Diary of Private Prayer* by John Baillie.

Arthur James for the extracts from *Hear Me, Lord* by Michael Walker.

Darton, Longman & Todd for the extract from *Listen Pilgrim* by C. W. Jones.

The United Reformed Church for the prayer from *The Soul of Prayer* by P. T. Forsyth.

James Clarke & Co for the passage from *What the Cross Means To Me*.

Hodder and Stoughton for the extracts from *Parish Prayers* by Frank Colquhoun, *A Diary of Prayer* by Elizabeth Goudge and *I've Got to Talk to Somebody* by Marjorie Holmes.

Fontana for the extracts from *The Carmelites* by George Bernanos and *Prayers for Help and Healing* by William Barclay.

Lutterworth Press for the prayer from *Prayers Old and New* by Henry S. Nash and the extracts from *Daily Prayer and Praise*.

A. R. Mowbray & Co for the prayer from *A Pilgrim's Book of Prayer* by Gilbert Shaw and the extracts from *The Prayer Manual* by F. B. MacNutt and *Prayers from Father Andrew* by K. E. Burne.

A. M. Heath & Co and the author for the extract from *Praying While You Work* by Hubert van Zeller.

Sheed & Ward for the extract from *Prayers, Poems and Songs* by Huub Oosterhuis.

J. M. Dent & Sons and the Trustees for the Copyrights of the late Dylan Thomas for the poem 'And Death shall have no dominion' from *Collected Poems* by Dylan Thomas.

Geoffrey Chapman for the extracts from *Lord, Make Me Truly Human* edited by Sister Vladima Schydlo OP.

SCM Press for the extracts from *A Kind of Praying* by Rex Chapman, *Out of the Whirlwind* by Rex Chapman, *More*

261

Contemporary Prayers edited by Caryl Micklem, *Contemporary Prayers for Public Worship* edited by Caryl Micklem, *The Cost of Discipleship* by Dietrich Bonhoeffer, *Prayers New and Old* by Arthur W. Robinson and *The Divine Companionship* by J. S. Hoyland.

Ligouri Publications for the prayers from *Prayers for the Time Being* by Max Pauli CSSR. Copyright 1971 Ligouri Publications, Ligouri, Missouri 63057.

Edward Arnold (Publishers) for the prayer from *Words for Worship* by C. R. Campling and M. Davis.

Rev. R. S. Ingamells for the extract which bears his name.

Granada Publishing for the poem by e. e. cummings from *Complete Poems* Volume II.

Alison and Busby for the extract from *Look Out, Whitey! Black Power's Gon' Get Your Mama* by Julius Lester.

Lorna Music Co. Ltd for the poem 'Come Down Lord from Your Heaven' (A Soho De Profundis) by Judith Piepe and Stephen Delft. Copyright 1966.

Morehouse-Barlow, 14 East 41st Street, New York 17 for the extracts from *The Covenant of Peace* compiled by John Pairman Brown and Richard L. York. Copyright 1971 by the Free Church of Berkeley.

The General Administration Committee of the Church of Scotland for the prayer from *Prayers for Family Worship*.

The Longman Group for the extracts from *A Cambridge Bede* by Milner-White.

Every effort has been made to trace the owners of copyright material, and we hope that no copyright has been infringed. Pardon is sought and apology made if the contrary be the case, and a correction will be made in any re-print of this book.